Ninja Foodi Smart Dual Heat

Air Fry Oven Cookbook

Super Easy, Healthy and Flavorful Dual Heat Air Fry Oven Recipes to Sear Crisp, Bake, Griddle and Air Roast Every Day| Enhanced with Color Pictures | **Camilla Martin**

TABLE OF CONTENTS

Introduction

Hello, I'm Camilla Martin, a mother of two wonderful children who have taught me the true value of health and family. My journey toward creating this recipe book began with a simple realization - my kids were at risk of obesity due to their love for junk food. The wake-up call came from our family doctor, and it was a turning point in our lives.

With a deep determination to improve our family's health, I embarked on a mission to transform our eating habits. I started taking my kids to exercise and discovered the incredible potential of the Ninja Foodi Dual Heat Air Fryer Oven. This remarkable appliance not only made healthy cooking a breeze but also empowered my children to actively participate in the kitchen.

In this cookbook, you'll find a wealth of culinary inspiration tailored to transform your family's eating habits. From wholesome breakfasts that kickstart your day with vitality to crispy, satisfying snacks that put those unhealthy cravings to rest, this book guides you through creating delicious, guilt-free desserts that delight the senses. Plus, explore an array of mouthwatering meat dishes and other hearty mains designed to tantalize your taste buds. Each recipe is thoughtfully crafted with easy-to-follow instructions and vibrant, enticing photographs, ensuring your journey to healthier, happier meals is as enjoyable as it is nourishing. It's time to embrace the Ninja Foodi Dual Heat Air Fryer Oven's potential and make your family's well-being a top priority.

Join me on this incredible journey to better health and happier family meals. By using the Ninja Foodi Dual Heat Air Fryer Oven and these recipes, my family was able to give up unhealthy junk food and rediscover the joy of home-cooked meals. I hope our story inspires you to do the same.

Invest in your family's health today, and together, let's create a world of delicious, nutritious possibilities with the Ninja Foodi Dual Heat Air Fryer Oven. Your health is worth it, and your family's happiness is too. Happy cooking!

With love and wellness,
Camilla Martin

CHAPTER 1

BREAKFAST

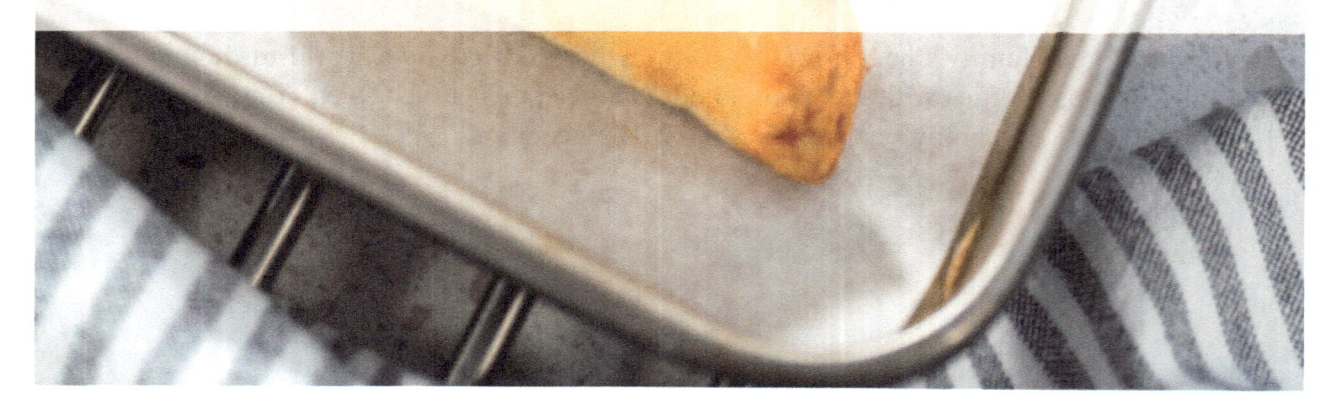

Egg and Bacon Muffins

PREP TIME: 5 minutes
COOK TIME: 15 minutes

2 eggs
1 tbsp. green pesto
5 ounces (142 g) cooked bacon
3 ounces (85 g) shredded Cheddar cheese
1 scallion, chopped
Salt and ground black pepper, to taste

1. Install rack in bottom position, then close door. Select BAKE, set temperature to 350°F, and set time to 15 minutes. Press the setting dial to begin preheating.
2. While unit is preheating, line a cupcake tin with parchment paper.
3. Beat the eggs with black pepper, salt, and pesto in a small bowl. Mix in the cheese.
4. Pour the egg mixture into the cupcake tin and top with the bacon and scallion.
5. When unit has preheated, open door and place the cupcake tin onto the center of the rack. Close door to begin cooking, until the egg is set.
6. When cooking is complete, carefully remove the muffins from the oven. Allow muffins to cool for 5 minutes before serving.

Breakfast Creamy Donuts

PREP TIME: 10 minutes
COOK TIME: 10 minutes

4 tbsps. butter, softened and divided
2 large egg yolks
2¼ cups plain flour
½ cup sour cream
½ cup sugar
⅓ cup caster sugar
1½ tsps. baking powder
1 pinch baking soda
1 tsp. cinnamon
1 tsp. salt

1. Mix together sugar and butter in a small bowl and beat until a crumbly mixture is formed.
2. Whisk in the egg yolks and beat until well combined.
3. Sift together the flour, baking powder, baking soda and salt in another bowl.
4. Add the flour mixture and sour cream to the sugar mixture.
5. Mix well to form a dough and refrigerate it.
6. Roll the dough into 2-inch thickness and cut into donuts with a donut cutter.
7. Coat both sides of the donuts with the melted butter. Place the donuts on a greased baking pan.
8. Install SearPlate in the bottom level of the unit, then close the door. Select RAPID BAKE, set temperature to 350°F, and set the time to 10 minutes. Press the setting dial to begin preheating.
9. When unit has preheated, open the door, carefully remove the SearPlate with oven mitts, and place on top of the oven. Carefully place the baking pan on the SearPlate. Reinstall the SearPlate in the bottom level of the unit and close the door to begin cooking, until golden brown.
10. When cooking is complete, remove the SearPlate. Sprinkle the donuts with the cinnamon and caster sugar to serve.

Homemade Vegetarian Pizza

Serves 1

PREP TIME: 10 minutes
COOK TIME: 7 minutes

Canola oil for rubbing
1 (7-ounce, 198 g) store-bought pizza dough, rolled into an 8-inch circle
¼ cup sliced mushrooms
¼ cup chopped green bell pepper
⅔ cup shredded mozzarella cheese
¼ cup traditional pizza sauce
1 tsp. minced garlic
Crushed red pepper flakes, for garnish

1. Install SearPlate in the bottom level of the unit, then close door. Select FRESH PIZZA, set temperature to 500°F, and set time to 7 minutes. Press the setting dial to begin preheating.
2. While unit is preheating, transfer the pizza dough to a sheet of parchment paper.
3. Brush the crust with pizza sauce, leaving about a 1-inch border uncovered. Sprinkle on the garlic, top with the mozzarella cheese, and evenly scatter the green bell pepper and mushrooms over the pizza.
4. Gently rub canola oil onto the outer edge of the dough.
5. When unit has preheated, transfer the pizza on the parchment paper to the hot SearPlate. Close door to begin cooking.
6. After 4 minutes of cooking, open door and carefully pull the parchment paper out from under the pizza, allowing the pizza to go directly onto the SearPlate. Close door to finish cooking.
7. When cooking is complete, carefully remove pizza from the hot SearPlate. Let pizza cool for 5 minutes then garnish with red pepper flakes. Enjoy!

Fluffy Cheese Omelet

Serves 2

PREP TIME: 10 minutes
COOK TIME: 12 minutes

Cooking spray
1 tsp. canola oil
4 eggs
1 large onion, sliced
⅛ cup mozzarella cheese, grated
⅛ cup cheddar cheese, grated
¼ tsp. soy sauce
Freshly ground black pepper, to taste

1. Spray a 8-inch baking pan with cooking spray.
2. In a skillet, heat the canola oil over medium heat and add the onion. Cook for 5-6 minutes, until tender.
3. Install rack in bottom position, then close door. Select BAKE, set temperature to 360°F, and set time to 6 minutes. Press the setting dial to begin preheating.
4. While unit is preheating, add the cooked onions to the greased baking pan. Pour the egg mixture and top evenly with cheese.
5. When unit has preheated, open door and place the baking pan onto the center of the rack. Close door to begin cooking, until the egg is set.
6. When cooking is complete, carefully remove the baking pan from the oven. Let cool for 5 minutes before serving.

Tomato Basil Pizza

PREP TIME: 5 minutes
COOK TIME: 7 minutes

2 tbsps canola oil
1 (12-inch) reduced-sodium prebaked pizza crust
1 cup shredded part-skim low-moisture mozzarella cheese
1 cup no-salt-added tomato sauce
¼ medium red onion, finely chopped
1 garlic clove, minced

1 tsp. dried oregano
1 tsp. dried basil
½ tsp freshly ground black pepper
¼ cup no-salt-added tomato paste
1 cup fresh basil leaves, chopped, for serving

1. In a medium skillet, heat the canola oil over low heat. Add the garlic and onion and stir for 1 minute, or until fragrant. Add the dried basil, oregano, pepper, tomato sauce, and tomato paste. Simmer for 10 minutes. Set aside.
2. Install SearPlate in the bottom level of the unit, then close door. Select FRESH PIZZA, set temperature to 500°F, and set time to 7 minutes. Press the setting dial to begin preheating.
3. While unit is preheating, place the pizza dough to a sheet of parchment paper. Top with the sauce. Sprinkle on the mozzarella cheese.
4. Then use a pastry brush or your fingers to gently rub canola oil onto the outer edge of the dough.
5. When unit has preheated, transfer the pizza on the parchment paper to the hot SearPlate. Close door to begin cooking.
6. After 4 minutes of cooking, open door and carefully pull the parchment paper out from under the pizza, allowing the pizza to go directly onto the SearPlate. Close door to finish cooking.
7. When cooking is complete, carefully remove pizza from the hot SearPlate. Let pizza cool for 5 minutes before cutting into 3 wedges. Top each wedge with ⅓ cup of basil and serve.

Quick Blueberry Muffins

PREP TIME: 10 minutes
COOK TIME: 16 minutes

1⅓ cups flour
½ cup sugar
2 tsps. baking powder
¼ tsp. salt
⅓ cup canola oil

1 egg
½ cup milk
⅔ cup blueberries, fresh or frozen and thawed

1. Install rack in bottom position, then close door. Select BAKE, set temperature to 330°F, and set time to 16 minutes. Press the setting dial to begin preheating.
2. While unit is preheating, stir together flour, sugar, baking powder, and salt in a medium bowl.
3. In a separate bowl, combine the canola oil, egg, and milk and mix well.
4. Add the egg mixture to dry ingredients and stir just until moistened.
5. Gently stir in the blueberries.
6. Spoon the batter evenly into parchment-paper-lined muffin cups. Place the muffin cups on a baking pan.
7. When unit has preheated, open door and place the baking pan on the rack. Close door to begin cooking.
8. After 16 minutes, check muffins for doneness by sticking a toothpick in the center of the muffins. If it comes out clean, remove from oven. Serve immediately.

Creamy Tomato Casserole

PREP TIME: 5 minutes
COOK TIME: 30 minutes

5 eggs
3 tbsps. chunky tomato sauce
2 tbsps. heavy cream
2 tbsps. grated Parmesan cheese, plus more for topping

1 Install rack in bottom position, then close door. Select BAKE, set temperature to 350°F, and set time to 30 minutes. Press the setting dial to begin preheating.

2. While unit is preheating, combine the eggs and cream in a medium bowl.

3. Mix in the tomato sauce and add the cheese. Stir to combine well.

4. Spread the mixture into a glass baking dish.

5. When unit has preheated, open door and place the baking dish onto the center of the rack. Close door to begin cooking, until the egg is set.

6. When cooking is complete, carefully remove dish from the oven. Top with extra cheese and serve.

Broccoli Cheese Quiche

Serves 2

PREP TIME: 10 minutes
COOK TIME: 40 minutes

cooking spray
3 large carrots, peeled and diced
1 large broccoli, chopped into florets
1 cup cheddar cheese, grated
2 large eggs
¼ cup feta cheese
1 tsp. dried rosemary

1 tsp. dried thyme
Salt and black pepper, to taste

1. Grease a quiche dish with cooking spray.

2. Place the broccoli and carrots into a food steamer and cook for about 20 minutes until soft.

3. Install rack in bottom position, then close door. Select BAKE, set temperature to 360°F, and set time to 20 minutes. Press the setting dial to begin preheating.

4. While unit is preheating, whisk together eggs with milk, dried herbs, salt and black pepper in a small bowl.

5. Place the steamed vegetables at the bottom of the quiche dish and top with tomatoes and cheese. Pour the egg mixture over.

6. When unit has preheated, open door and place the dish onto the center of the rack. Close door to begin cooking.

7. When cooking is complete, carefully remove dish from the oven. Serve warm.

Pita and Pepperoni Pizza

Serves 1

PREP TIME: 10 minutes
COOK TIME: 7 minutes

1 tsp. canola oil
1 tbsp. pizza sauce
1 pita bread
6 pepperoni slices
¼ cup grated Mozzarella cheese
¼ tsp. garlic powder
¼ tsp. dried oregano

1. Install SearPlate in the bottom level of the unit, then close door. Select FRESH PIZZA, set temperature to 500°F, and set time to 7 minutes. Press the setting dial to begin preheating.
2. While unit is preheating, lightly coat the pita bread with canola oil and spread the pizza sauce over. Then top with the pepperoni slices, followed by the Mozzarella cheese.
3. Season with garlic powder and oregano to taste.
4. When unit has preheated, transfer the pizza to the hot SearPlate. Close door to begin cooking.
5. When cooking is complete, carefully remove pizza from the hot SearPlate. Let pizza cool for 5 minutes, then serve.

Sweet Potato Hash

Serves 6

PREP TIME: 10 minutes
COOK TIME: 15 minutes

2 tbsps. canola oil
2 large sweet potatoes, cut into small cubes
2 slices bacon, cut into small pieces
1 tbsp. smoked paprika
1 tsp. dried dill weed
1 tsp. sea salt
1 tsp. ground black pepper

1. Install SearPlate in the bottom level of the unit, then close door. Select GRIDDLE, set temperature to 400°F, and set time to 15 minutes. Press the setting dial to begin preheating.
2. While unit is preheating, mix together sweet potatoes, bacon, canola oil, paprika, salt, black pepper and dill in a large bowl.
3. When unit has preheated, open door, carefully transfer the mixture to the hot SearPlate.
4. Reinstall the SearPlate in the bottom level of the unit and close the door to begin cooking, stirring in between.
5. When cooking is complete, remove the sweet potato hash from the SearPlate, and serve hot.

CHAPTER 2

SANDWICHES

Mixed Greens Sandwich

PREP TIME: 15 minutes
COOK TIME: 10-11 minutes

2 tsps. canola oil
1½ cups chopped mixed greens
2 garlic cloves, thinly sliced
4 slices low-sodium whole-wheat bread
2 slices low-sodium low-fat Swiss cheese
Cooking spray

1. Install SearPlate in the bottom level of the unit, then close door. Select GRIDDLE, set temperature to 400°F, and set time to 6 minutes. Press the setting dial to begin preheating.
2. While unit is preheating, mix the greens, garlic, and canola oil in a skillet and cook on medium heat for 4 to 5 minutes, stirring once, until the vegetables are tender. Drain, if necessary.
3. Make 2 sandwiches, distributing half of the greens and 1 slice of Swiss cheese between 2 slices of bread. Lightly spray the outsides of the sandwiches with cooking spray.
4. When unit has preheated, open door, carefully transfer the sandwiches to the hot SearPlate.
5. Reinstall the SearPlate in the bottom level of the unit and close the door to begin cooking, turning with tongs halfway through, until the bread is toasted and the cheese melts.
6. When cooking is complete, remove the sandwiches from the SearPlate. Cut each sandwich in half and serve.

Bacon Cheese Sandwich

PREP TIME: 5 minutes
COOK TIME: 7 minutes

Cooking spray
4 slices of bread
1 tbsp. butter, softened
6 slices bacon, cooked
2 slices mild cheddar cheese
2 slices mozzarella cheese

1. Install SearPlate in the bottom level of the unit, then close door. Select GRIDDLE, set temperature to 375°F, and set time to 7 minutes. Press the setting dial to begin preheating.
2. Spread butter onto one side of each bread slice.
3. When unit has preheated, open door, carefully transfer the sandwiches to the hot SearPlate. Layer with cheddar cheese, followed by bacon, mozzarella cheese and close with the other bread slice. Spray with cooking spray.
4. Reinstall the SearPlate in the bottom level of the unit and close the door to begin cooking, flipping halfway.
5. When cooking is complete, remove the sandwiches from the SearPlate, and serve warm.

Cheesy Chicken Sandwich

PREP TIME: 10 minutes
COOK TIME: 7 minutes

1 hamburger bun
⅓ cup chicken, cooked and shredded
2 Mozzarella slices
¼ cup shredded cabbage
1 tsp. canola oil
1 tsp. mayonnaise

2 tsps. butter, melted
½ tsp. balsamic vinegar
¼ tsp. garlic powder
¼ tsp. smoked paprika
¼ tsp. black pepper
Pinch of salt

1. Install SearPlate in the bottom level of the unit, then close door. Select GRIDDLE, set temperature to 370°F, and set time to 7 minutes. Press the setting dial to begin preheating.
2. While unit is preheating, brush some butter onto the outside of the hamburger bun.
3. In a small bowl, coat the cooked chicken with the garlic powder, salt, pepper, and paprika.
4. In a separate bowl, stir together the canola oil, mayonnaise, cabbage, and balsamic vinegar to make coleslaw.
5. Slice the bun in two. Start building the sandwich, starting with the chicken, followed by the Mozzarella, the coleslaw, and finally the top bun.
6. When unit has preheated, open door, carefully transfer the sandwich to the hot SearPlate.
7. Reinstall the SearPlate in the bottom level of the unit and close the door to begin cooking.
8. When cooking is complete, remove the sandwich from the SearPlate, and serve warm.

Veggie Pita Sandwich

PREP TIME: 10 minutes
COOK TIME: 10 minutes

1 tsp. canola oil
2 low-sodium whole-wheat pita breads, halved crosswise
1 baby eggplant, peeled and chopped
1 red bell pepper, sliced

½ cup diced red onion
½ cup shredded carrot
⅓ cup low-fat Greek yogurt
½ tsp. dried tarragon

1. Install SearPlate in the bottom level of the unit, then close the door. Select AIR ROAST, set temperature to 400°F, and set time to 8 minutes. Press the setting dial to begin preheating.
2. Stir together the eggplant, red bell pepper, red onion, carrot, and canola oil in a medium bowl.
3. When unit has preheated, open door and use oven mitts to remove SearPlate and place it on top of oven. Transfer the vegetable mixture to the SearPlate.
4. Reinstall the SearPlate in the bottom level of the unit. Close door to begin cooking, until the vegetables are tender.
5. Meanwhile, in a small bowl, thoroughly mix the yogurt and tarragon until well combined.
6. When cooking is complete, carefully remove SearPlate from oven with oven mitts.
7. Stir the yogurt mixture into the vegetables. Stuff one-fourth of this mixture into each pita pocket.
8. Place the sandwiches on the SearPlate and install in the bottom level of the unit, then close the door. Select GRIDDLE, set temperature to 400°F, and set time to 2 minutes. Skip the preheating and begin cooking, until the bread is toasted.
9. When cooking is complete, carefully remove SearPlate from oven and serve immediately.

Bacon and Pepper Sandwich

Serves 4

PREP TIME: 10 minutes
COOK TIME: 6 minutes

nonstick spray
2 tbsps. honey
⅓ cup spicy barbecue sauce
2 pita pockets, cut in half
½ cup torn butter lettuce leaves
6 slices cooked bacon, cut into thirds

1 red bell pepper, sliced
1 yellow bell pepper, sliced
1 tomato, sliced

1. In a small bowl, combine the barbecue sauce and honey. Brush this sauce mixture lightly onto the bacon slices and the pepper slices.
2. Remove Air Fry Basket from oven. Select AIR FRY, set temperature to 350°F, and set time to 6 minutes. Press the setting dial to begin preheating.
3. While unit is preheating, arrange the peppers in the basket, making sure they are not crowding each other. Spray with nonstick spray.
4. When unit has preheated, open door, install the SearPlate in the bottom level of the unit and the basket in the top level of the unit. Close door to begin cooking.
5. After 4 minutes, shake the basket, add the bacon. Return basket to oven and cook for an additional 2 minutes, the bacon is browned and the peppers are tender.
6. When cooking is complete, carefully remove basket from the oven.
7. Fill the pita halves with the bacon, peppers, any remaining barbecue sauce, lettuce, and tomatoes, and enjoy.

Baked Cheese Sandwich

Serves 2

PREP TIME: 5 minutes
COOK TIME: 6 minutes

2 tbsps. mayonnaise
8 slices hot capicola
4 thick slices Brie cheese
4 thick slices sourdough bread

1. Install SearPlate in the bottom level of the unit, then close door. Select GRIDDLE, set temperature to 375°F, and set time to 6 minutes. Press the setting dial to begin preheating.
2. While unit is preheating, spread the mayonnaise on one side of each slice of bread.
3. When unit has preheated, open door, place 2 slices of bread on the hot SearPlate, mayonnaise-side down. Place the slices of Brie and capicola on the bread and cover with the remaining two slices of bread, mayonnaise-side up.
4. Reinstall the SearPlate in the bottom level of the unit and close the door to begin cooking, until the cheese has melted.
5. When cooking is complete, remove the sandwiches from the SearPlate, and serve immediately.

Tuna Muffin Sandwich

PREP TIME: 8 minutes
COOK TIME: 6 minutes

1 (6-ounce / 170-g) can chunk light tuna, drained
3 English muffins, split with a fork
6 thin slices Provolone or Muenster cheese
¼ cup mayonnaise
2 tbsps. mustard
1 tbsp. lemon juice
2 green onions, minced
3 tbsps. softened butter

1. Install SearPlate in the bottom level of the unit, then close door. Select GRIDDLE, set temperature to 390°F, and set time to 6 minutes. Press the setting dial to begin preheating.
2. While unit is preheating, in a small bowl, combine the tuna, mustard, mayonnaise, lemon juice, and green onions. Set aside.
3. Butter the cut side of the English muffins.
4. When unit has preheated, open door, carefully transfer the muffins to the hot SearPlate, butter-side up.
5. Reinstall the SearPlate in the bottom level of the unit and close the door to begin cooking.
6. After 4 minutes, open door and top each muffin with one slice of cheese. Close door to finish cooking.
7. When cooking is complete, remove the muffins from the SearPlate. Top with the tuna mixture and serve warm.

Cheese Tiny Shrimp Sandwich

PREP TIME: 10 minutes
COOK TIME: 6 minutes

2 tbsps. softened butter
1¼ cups shredded Colby, Cheddar, or Havarti cheese
1 (6-ounce / 170-g) can tiny shrimp, drained
4 slices whole grain or whole-wheat bread
3 tbsps. mayonnaise
2 tbsps. minced green onion

1. Install SearPlate in the bottom level of the unit, then close door. Select GRIDDLE, set temperature to 400°F, and set time to 6 minutes. Press the setting dial to begin preheating.
2. While unit is preheating, combine the cheese, shrimp, mayonnaise and green onion in a medium bowl, and mix well.
3. Spread this shrimp mixture on two of the slices of bread. Top with the other slices of bread to make two sandwiches. Spread the sandwiches lightly with butter.
4. When unit has preheated, open door, carefully transfer the sandwiches to the hot SearPlate.
5. Reinstall the SearPlate in the bottom level of the unit and close the door to begin cooking, until the bread is browned and crisp and the cheese is melted.
6. When cooking is complete, remove the sandwiches from the SearPlate, then cut in half and serve warm.

Chicken Pita Sandwich

PREP TIME: 10 minutes	2 boneless, skinless chicken breasts, cut into 1-inch cubes
COOK TIME: 10 minutes	1 red bell pepper, sliced
	1 small red onion, sliced
	⅓ cup Italian salad dressing, divided
	½ tsp. dried thyme
	4 pita pockets, split
	2 cups torn butter lettuce
	1 cup chopped cherry tomatoes

1. Install SearPlate in the bottom level of the unit, then close the door. Select AIR ROAST, set temperature to 400°F, and set time to 10 minutes. Press the setting dial to begin preheating.

2. While unit is preheating, add the chicken, onion, and bell pepper in a medium bowl. Drizzle with 1 tbsp. of the Italian salad dressing, add the thyme, and toss well.

3. When unit has preheated, open door and use oven mitts to remove SearPlate and place it on top of oven. Transfer the chicken mixture to the SearPlate.

4. Reinstall the SearPlate in the bottom level of the unit. Close door to begin cooking, until the chicken is 165ºF (74ºC) on a food thermometer, stirring once during cooking time.

5. When cooking is complete, carefully remove SearPlate from oven with oven mitts. Transfer the chicken and vegetables to a bowl and toss with the remaining salad dressing.

6. Assemble sandwiches with the pita pockets, butter lettuce, and cherry tomatoes. Serve immediately.

Sweet Corn and Bell Pepper Sandwich

PREP TIME: 15 minutes	2 tbsps. butter, softened
COOK TIME: 7 minutes	4 bread slices, trimmed and cut horizontally
	1 cup sweet corn kernels
	1 roasted green bell pepper, chopped
	¼ cup barbecue sauce

1. Install SearPlate in the bottom level of the unit, then close door. Select GRIDDLE, set temperature to 375°F, and set time to 7 minutes. Press the setting dial to begin preheating.

2. While unit is preheating, heat butter in a skillet on medium heat and add the corn.

3. Sauté for about 2 minutes and transfer to a bowl.

4. Add the bell pepper and barbecue sauce to the corn.

5. Spread corn mixture on one side of 2 bread slices and top with remaining slices.

6. When unit has preheated, open door. carefully transfer the sandwiches to the hot SearPlate.

7. Reinstall the SearPlate in the bottom level of the unit and close the door to begin cooking, until the vegetables are tender.

8. When cooking is complete, remove the sandwiches from the SearPlate, and serve.

CHAPTER 3

FISH AND SEAFOOD

Paprika Shrimp

PREP TIME: 10 minutes
COOK TIME: 10 minutes

1 pound tiger shrimp
2 tbsps. canola oil
½ tsp. smoked paprika
Salt, to taste

1. Install SearPlate in the bottom level of the unit, then close the door. Select AIR ROAST, set temperature to 390°F, and set time to 10 minutes. Press the setting dial to begin preheating.
2. While unit is preheating, mix all the ingredients in a large bowl until well combined.
3. When unit has preheated, open door and use oven mitts to remove SearPlate and place it on top of oven. Transfer shrimp to the SearPlate.
4. Reinstall the SearPlate in the bottom level of the unit. Close door to begin cooking, flipping halfway through cooking.
5. When cooking is complete, carefully remove SearPlate from oven with oven mitts. Serve warm.

Crispy Cod with Asparagus

PREP TIME: 15 minutes
COOK TIME: 20 minutes

2 (6-ounces) boneless cod fillets
2 tbsps. fresh parsley, roughly chopped
2 tbsps. fresh dill, roughly chopped
1 bunch asparagus
1 tsp. dried basil
1½ tbsps. fresh lemon juice
1 tbsp. canola oil
Salt and black pepper, to taste

1. Install SearPlate in the bottom level of the unit, then close door. Select SEAR CRISP, set temperature to 325°F, and set time to 20 minutes. Press the setting dial to begin preheating.
2. While unit is preheating, mix lemon juice, oil, basil, salt, and black pepper in a small bowl.
3. Combine the cod and asparagus with the oil mixture.
4. When unit has preheated, open door, carefully remove the SearPlate with oven mitts and place on top of oven. Place the cod and asparagus on the SearPlate.
5. Reinstall the SearPlate in the bottom level of the unit and close the door to begin cooking, until the fish is easy flaked by forks and the asparagus is tender.
6. When cooking is complete, remove from the SearPlate. Serve the cod warm with asparagus.

Broiled Salmon

PREP TIME: 5 minutes
COOK TIME: 10 minutes

1 tbsp. canola oil
2 (6-ounces) salmon fillets
Salt and black pepper, as required

1. Season each salmon fillet with salt and black pepper and drizzle with canola oil.
2. Remove SearPlate from oven. Select BROIL, set temperature to LO, and set time to 10 minutes.
3. Place the salmon fillets in the SearPlate. Open door and install the SearPlate in the bottom level of the unit. Close door and begin cooking, flipping halfway through cooking.
4. When cooking is complete, carefully remove SearPlate from the oven. Transfer the salmon fillets onto the serving plates. Serve warm.

Creamy Tuna Cakes

PREP TIME: 15 minutes
COOK TIME: 12 minutes

nonstick spray
1½ tbsps. mayonnaise
1½ tbsps. almond flour
1 tbsp. fresh lemon juice
1 tsp. dried dill
1 tsp. garlic powder
½ tsp. onion powder

2 (6-ounces) cans tuna, drained
Pinch of salt and ground black pepper

1. Mix the tuna, mayonnaise, almond flour, lemon juice, dill, and spices in a large bowl.
2. Shape the tuna mixture into 4 equal-sized patties.
3. Remove Air Fry Basket from oven. Select AIR FRY, set temperature to 400°F, and set time to 25 minutes. Press the setting dial to begin preheating.
4. While unit is preheating, arrange patties in the basket in a single layer. Spray with nonstick spray.
5. When unit has preheated, open door, install the SearPlate in the bottom level of the unit and the basket in the top level of the unit. Close door to begin cooking, flipping halfway through cooking.
6. When cooking is complete, carefully remove basket from the oven. Transfer the tuna cakes to serving plates and serve warm.

Roasted Cod with Sesame Seeds

PREP TIME: 5 minutes
COOK TIME: 8 minutes

Cooking spray
6 ounces (170 g) fresh cod fillet
1 tbsp. reduced-sodium soy sauce
2 tsps. honey
1 tsp. sesame seeds

1. In a small bowl, combine the soy sauce and honey.
2. Install SearPlate in the bottom level of the unit, then close the door. Select AIR ROAST, set temperature to 400°F, and set time to 8 minutes. Press the setting dial to begin preheating.
3. When unit has preheated, open door and use oven mitts to remove SearPlate and place it on top of oven. Transfer cod to the SearPlate and brush with the soy mixture, and sprinkle sesame seeds on top. Spray with cooking spray.
4. Reinstall the SearPlate in the bottom level of the unit. Close door to begin cooking until opaque, flipping halfway through cooking.
5. When cooking is complete, carefully remove SearPlate from oven with oven mitts. Let cool on a wire rack for 5 minutes before serving.

Cajun Spiced Salmon

Serves 2

PREP TIME: 10 minutes
COOK TIME: 10 minutes

Cooking spray
2 (7-ounces) (¾-inch thick) salmon fillets
1 tbsp. Cajun seasoning
1 tbsp. fresh lemon juice
½ tsp. coconut sugar

1. Season the salmon evenly with Cajun seasoning and coconut sugar. Spray with cooking spray.
2. Remove SearPlate from oven. Select BROIL, set temperature to LO, and set time to 10 minutes.
3. Place the salmon in the SearPlate. Open door and install the SearPlate in the bottom level of the unit. Close door and begin cooking, flipping halfway through cooking.
4. When cooking is complete, carefully remove SearPlate from the oven. Drizzle with the lemon juice and serve hot.

Crispy Scallops

PREP TIME: 15 minutes COOK TIME: 6 minutes	18 sea scallops, cleaned and patted very dry ½ egg ¼ cup cornflakes, crushed ⅛ cup all-purpose flour 1 tbsp. 2% milk ½ tsp. paprika Salt and black pepper, as required

1. Mix the flour, paprika, salt, and black pepper in a bowl.
2. Whisk the egg with milk in another bowl and place the cornflakes in a third bowl.
3. Coat each scallop with the flour mixture, dip into the egg mixture and finally, dredge in the cornflakes.
4. Install SearPlate in the bottom level of the unit, then close the door. Select AIR ROAST, set temperature to 400°F, and set time to 6 minutes. Press the setting dial to begin preheating.
5. When unit has preheated, open door and use oven mitts to remove SearPlate and place it on top of oven. Transfer scallops to the SearPlate.
6. Reinstall the SearPlate in the bottom level of the unit. Close door to begin cooking, flipping halfway through cooking.
7. When cooking is complete, carefully remove SearPlate from oven with oven mitts. Transfer the scallops to a platter and serve hot.

Lemony Shrimp and Zucchini

PREP TIME: 15 minutes COOK TIME: 20 minutes	1 pound (454 g) extra-large raw shrimp, peeled and deveined 2 medium zucchinis (about 8 ounces / 227 g each), halved lengthwise and cut into ½-inch-thick slices 1½ tbsps. canola oil Juice of ½ lemon 1 tbsp. chopped fresh dill 1 tbsp. chopped fresh mint ½ tsp. garlic salt 1½ tsps. dried oregano ⅛ tsp. crushed red pepper flakes (optional)

1. In a large bowl, combine the shrimp, zucchinis, oil, garlic salt, oregano, and pepper flakes (if using) and toss to coat well.
2. Install SearPlate in the bottom level of the unit, then close the door. Select AIR ROAST, set temperature to 400°F, and set time to 20 minutes. Press the setting dial to begin preheating.
3. When unit has preheated, open door and use oven mitts to remove SearPlate and place it on top of oven. Place the shrimp on the left side and the zucchini on the right.
4. Reinstall the SearPlate in the bottom level of the unit. Close door to begin cooking, flipping halfway through cooking.
5. When cooking is complete, carefully remove SearPlate from oven with oven mitts. Transfer the shrimp and zucchini to a serving bowl. Top with the lemon juice, mint, and dill and serve.

Shrimp Green Casserole

PREP TIME: 15 minutes
COOK TIME: 22 minutes

Cooking spray
2 tbsps. sesame oil
1 pound (454 g) shrimp, cleaned and deveined
2 green bell pepper, sliced
2 cups cauliflower, cut into florets
1 shallot, sliced
1 cup tomato paste

1. Spritz a baking pan with cooking spray.
2. Arrange the shrimp and vegetables in the baking pan. Then drizzle with the sesame oil and pour in the tomato paste.
3. Install rack in bottom position, then close door. Select BAKE, set temperature to 360°F, and set time to 22 minutes. Press the setting dial to begin preheating.
4. When unit has preheated, open door and place pan onto the center of the rack. Close door to begin cooking.
5. After 10 minutes, open door and stir with a large spoon. Close door to finish cooking.
6. When cooking is complete, carefully remove pan from the oven. Serve warm.

Cod with Shrimps and Pasta

PREP TIME: 20 minutes
COOK TIME: 22 minutes

14 ounces pasta
4 (4-ounces) cod steaks
½ pound mushrooms, chopped
8 large shrimps, peeled and deveined
2 tbsps. fresh parsley, chopped
4 tbsps. pesto, divided
2 tbsps. canola oil
2 tbsps. fresh lemon juice

1. Grease a baking dish lightly.
2. Cook pasta in a large pan of salted water for about 10 minutes.
3. Meanwhile, spread the pesto in the bottom of a baking dish.
4. Arrange the cod steaks and mushrooms over pesto and drizzle evenly with canola oil.
5. Top with shrimps and sprinkle with lemon juice and parsley.
6. Install rack in bottom position and close the door. Select AIR ROAST, set temperature to 400°F, and set time to 12 minutes. Press the setting dial to begin preheating.
7. When unit is preheated, open the door and place the dish onto the center of the rack. Close door to begin cooking.
8. When cooking is complete, carefully remove dish from the oven. Serve the cod and shrimps with pasta and enjoy.

CHAPTER 4

BEEF

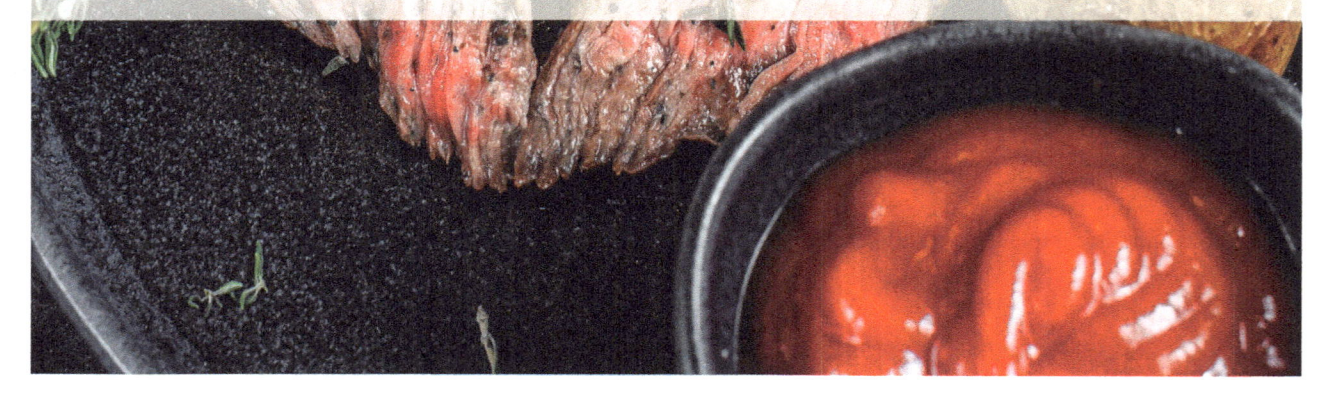

Simple New York Strip Steak

PREP TIME: 10 minutes
COOK TIME: 10 minutes

1 tsp. canola oil
1 (9½-ounces) New York strip steak
Crushed red pepper flakes, to taste
Salt and black pepper, to taste

1. Install SearPlate in the bottom level of the unit, then close door. Select SEAR CRISP, set temperature to 400°F, and set time to 10 minutes. Press the setting dial to begin preheating.
2. While unit is preheating, rub the steak generously with red pepper flakes, salt and black pepper and coat with canola oil.
3. When unit has preheated, open door, carefully remove the SearPlate with oven mitts and place on top of oven. Place the steak on the SearPlate.
4. Reinstall the SearPlate in the bottom level of the unit and close the door to begin cooking. After 10 minutes, begin to check steak for doneness. If further doneness is desired, leave in oven.
5. When cooking is complete, remove the steak from the SearPlate and cut into desired size slices to serve.

Rubbed Rib Steak

PREP TIME: 10 minutes
COOK TIME: 15 minutes

2 cup steak rub
2 lbs. rib steak
1 tbsp. canola oil

1. Install SearPlate in the bottom level of the unit, then close door. Select SEAR CRISP, set temperature to 400°F, and set time to 15 minutes. Press the setting dial to begin preheating.
2. While unit is preheating, rub the steak generously with steak rub, salt and black pepper, and coat with canola oil.
3. When unit has preheated, open door, carefully remove the SearPlate with oven mitts and place on top of oven. Place the steak on the SearPlate.
4. Reinstall the SearPlate in the bottom level of the unit and close the door to begin cooking, flipping once in between.
5. When cooking is complete, make sure the steak is cooked through with a thermometer. The internal temperature should read 145°F. Remove the steak from the SearPlate and cut into desired size slices to serve.

(Note: To prepare the Steak Rub - 2 tbsps. fresh cracked black pepper, 2 tbsps. kosher salt, 2 tbsps. paprika, 1 tbsp. crushed red pepper flakes, 1 tbsp. crushed coriander seeds (not ground), 1 tbsp. garlic powder, 1 tbsp. onion powder, 2 tsps. cayenne pepper. Mix all ingredients in a medium bowl and stir well to combine.)

Tasty Beef Stuffed Bell Peppers

PREP TIME: 20 minutes
COOK TIME: 26 minutes

½ medium onion, chopped
1 pound lean ground beef
4 bell peppers, tops and seeds removed
½ cup jasmine rice, cooked
⅔ cup light Mexican cheese, shredded and divided
8 ounces tomato sauce, divided

1 tsp. canola oil
2 garlic cloves, minced
1 tsp. dried basil, crushed
1 tsp. garlic salt
½ tsp. red chili powder
Ground black pepper, as required
2 tsps. Worcestershire sauce

1. Heat the canola oil in a medium skillet over medium heat and add the onion and garlic.
2. Sauté for 5 minutes and add the ground beef, basil and spices.
3. Cook for about 10 minutes and drain off the excess grease from skillet.
4. Stir in the rice, half of the cheese, ⅔ of the tomato sauce and Worcestershire sauce and combine well.
5. Evenly stuff the beef mixture in each bell pepper.
6. Install SearPlate in the bottom level of the unit, then close the door. Select AIR ROAST, set temperature to 400°F, and set time to 11 minutes. Press the setting dial to begin preheating.
7. When unit has preheated, open door and use oven mitts to remove SearPlate and place it on top of oven. Transfer the bell peppers to the SearPlate.
8. Reinstall the SearPlate in the bottom level of the unit. Close door to begin cooking.
9. After 7 minutes, open door and top with the remaining tomato sauce and cheese. Close door to finish cooking.
10. When cooking is complete, carefully remove SearPlate from oven with oven mitts. Serve warm.

Crispy Beef Bratwursts

PREP TIME: 5 minutes
COOK TIME: 12 minutes

4 (3-ounce / 85-g) beef bratwursts

1. Install SearPlate in the bottom level of the unit, then close door. Select SEAR CRISP, set temperature to 400°F, and set time to 12 minutes. Press the setting dial to begin preheating.
2. When unit has preheated, open door, carefully remove the SearPlate with oven mitts and place on top of oven. Place the beef bratwursts on the SearPlate.
3. Reinstall the SearPlate in the bottom level of the unit and close the door to begin cooking until crispy, turning once halfway through.
4. When cooking is complete, remove from the SearPlate and serve hot.

Spiced Roast Beef

PREP TIME: 10 minutes
COOK TIME: 35 minutes

2½ pounds beef eye of round roast, trimmed
2 tbsps. canola oil
½ tsp. garlic powder
½ tsp. onion powder
½ tsp. cayenne pepper
½ tsp. ground black pepper
Salt, to taste

1. Install SearPlate in the bottom level of the unit, then close door. Select SEAR CRISP, set temperature to 450°F, and set time to 35 minutes. Press the setting dial to begin preheating.
2. While unit is preheating, rub the roast generously with all the spices and coat with canola oil.
3. When unit has preheated, open door, carefully remove the SearPlate with oven mitts and place on top of oven. Place the roast on the SearPlate.
4. Reinstall the SearPlate in the bottom level of the unit and close the door to begin cooking.
5. When cooking is complete, make sure the roast is cooked through with a thermometer. The internal temperature should read 145°F or higher. Remove the roast from the SearPlate and cut into desired size slices and serve.

Beef Jerky

PREP TIME: 20 minutes
COOK TIME: 6 hours

1 pound bottom round beef, cut into thin strips
½ cup soy sauce
½ cup dark brown sugar
¼ cup Worcestershire sauce
1 tbsp. hickory liquid smoke
1 tbsp. chili pepper sauce

1 tsp. garlic powder
1 tsp. cayenne pepper
1 tsp. onion powder
½ tsp. smoked paprika
½ tsp. ground black pepper

1. Mix the brown sugar, all the sauces, liquid smoke, and spices in a medium bowl.
2. Coat the beef strips with this marinade generously and marinate overnight.
3. Remove Air Fry Basket from oven. Select DEHYDRATE, set temperature to 150°F, and set time to 6 hours.
4. Place the beef strips in the Air Fry Basket in a single layer. Open door and install the basket in the top position level of the unit. Close door and begin cooking, flipping halfway through cooking.
5. When cooking is complete, carefully remove basket from the oven. Enjoy!

Peppercorn Crusted Beef Tenderloin

PREP TIME: 5 minutes
COOK TIME: 20 minutes

2 tbsps. avocado oil
2 pounds (907 g) beef tenderloin
2 tsps. roasted garlic, minced
3 tbsps. ground 4-peppercorn blender

1. Install SearPlate in the bottom level of the unit, then close door. Select SEAR CRISP, set temperature to 450°F, and set time to 20 minutes. Press the setting dial to begin preheating.
2. While unit is preheating, remove any surplus fat from the beef tenderloin.
3. Combine the roasted garlic and avocado oil to apply to the tenderloin with a brush.
4. Spread out the peppercorns on a plate and roll the tenderloin in them, making sure they are covering and clinging to the meat.
5. When unit has preheated, open door, carefully remove the SearPlate with oven mitts and place on top of oven. Place the beef tenderloin on the SearPlate.
6. Reinstall the SearPlate in the bottom level of the unit and close the door to begin cooking, turning halfway through cooking. After 20 minutes, begin to check the tenderloin for doneness. If further doneness is desired, leave in oven.
7. When cooking is complete, remove the tenderloin from the SearPlate and let rest for ten minutes before slicing and serving.

Beef and Veggie Kebabs

Serves 4

PREP TIME: 20 minutes
COOK TIME: 12 minutes

1 pound sirloin steak, cut into 1-inch chunks Salt and black pepper, to taste
1 large bell pepper, seeded and cut into 1-inch pieces
8 ounces baby Bella mushrooms, stems removed
1 red onion, cut into 1-inch pieces
¼ cup canola oil
¼ cup soy sauce
1 tbsp. garlic, minced
1 tsp. coconut sugar
½ tsp. ground cumin

1. Mix the soy sauce, canola oil, garlic, coconut sugar, cumin, salt and black pepper in a large bowl.
2. Coat the steak cubes generously with marinade and refrigerate to marinate for 30 minutes.
3. Thread the steak cubes, mushrooms, bell pepper and onion onto metal skewers.
4. Install SearPlate in the bottom level of the unit, then close the door. Select AIR ROAST, set temperature to 390°F, and set time to 12 minutes. Press the setting dial to begin preheating.
5. When unit has preheated, open door and use oven mitts to remove SearPlate and place it on top of oven. Transfer the skewers to the SearPlate.
6. Reinstall the SearPlate in the bottom level of the unit. Close door to begin cooking, flipping once in between.
7. When cooking is complete, carefully remove SearPlate from oven with oven mitts. Serve hot.

Beef with Sliced Jalapeños

PREP TIME: 10 minutes
COOK TIME: 30 minutes

2 tbsps. extra-virgin canola oil
2 pounds (907 g) roast beef, at room temperature
2 jalapeño peppers, thinly sliced
1 tsp. sea salt flakes
1 tsp. ground black pepper
1 tsp. smoked paprika
Few dashes of liquid smoke

1. Install SearPlate in the bottom level of the unit, then close door. Select SEAR CRISP, set temperature to 450°F, and set time to 30 minutes. Press the setting dial to begin preheating.
2. While unit is preheating, pat the beef dry with kitchen towels.
3. Massage the canola oil, salt, black pepper and paprika into the meat. Cover with liquid smoke.
4. When unit has preheated, open door, carefully remove the SearPlate with oven mitts and place on top of oven. Place the beef on the SearPlate.
5. Reinstall the SearPlate in the bottom level of the unit and close the door to begin cooking, flipping once in between. After 30 minutes, begin to check beef for doneness. If further doneness is desired, leave in oven.
6. When cooking is complete, remove the beef from the SearPlate, serve topped with sliced jalapeños.

Crumbed Golden Filet Mignon

PREP TIME: 15 minutes
COOK TIME: 12 minutes

½ pound (227 g) filet mignon
1 small egg, whisked
½ cup bread crumbs
Sea salt and ground black pepper, to taste
½ tsp. cayenne pepper
1 tsp. dried rosemary
1 tsp. dried basil
1 tsp. dried thyme
1 tbsp. sesame oil

1. Install SearPlate in the bottom level of the unit, then close door. Select SEAR CRISP, set temperature to 380°F, and set time to 12 minutes. Press the setting dial to begin preheating.
2. While unit is preheating, cover the filet mignon with the salt, black pepper, cayenne pepper, rosemary, basil and thyme. Coat with sesame oil.
3. Put the egg in a shallow plate. Pour the bread crumbs in another plate.
4. Dip the filet mignon into the egg. Then roll it into the crumbs.
5. When unit has preheated, open door, carefully remove the SearPlate with oven mitts and place on top of oven. Place the steak on the SearPlate.
6. Reinstall the SearPlate in the bottom level of the unit and close the door to begin cooking. After 10 minutes, begin to check steak for doneness. If further doneness is desired, leave in oven.
7. When cooking is complete, remove the steak from the SearPlate and serve immediately.

CHAPTER 5

POULTRY

Seared Duck Breasts

PREP TIME: 15 minutes
COOK TIME: 20 minutes

2 (12-ounces) duck breasts
3 tbsps. canola oil
½ tsp. dried thyme, crushed
¼ tsp. star anise powder
Salt and ground black pepper, as required

1. Install SearPlate in the bottom level of the unit, then close door. Select SEAR CRISP, set temperature to 425°F, and set time to 20 minutes. Press the setting dial to begin preheating.
2. While unit is preheating, season the duck breasts generously with salt and black pepper.
3. When unit has preheated, open door, carefully remove the SearPlate with oven mitts and place on top of oven. Place the duck breasts on the SearPlate.
4. Reinstall the SearPlate in the bottom level of the unit and close the door to begin cooking.
5. After 10 minutes, open door and drizzle with canola oil. Season with thyme and star anise powder. Close door to finish cooking.
6. When cooking is complete, remove the duck breasts from the SearPlate and serve warm.

Spinach Stuffed Chicken Breasts

PREP TIME: 15 minutes
COOK TIME: 25 minutes

1 tbsp. canola oil
2 (4-ounces) skinless, boneless chicken breasts
1¾ ounces fresh spinach
¼ cup ricotta cheese, shredded
2 tbsps. cheddar cheese, grated
Salt and ground black pepper, as required
¼ tsp. paprika

1. Heat the canola oil in a medium skillet over medium heat and cook spinach for about 4 minutes.
2. Add the ricotta cheese and cook for about 1 minute.
3. Cut the slits in each chicken breast horizontally and stuff with the spinach mixture.
4. Season each chicken breast evenly with salt and black pepper and top with cheddar cheese and paprika.
5. Remove SearPlate from oven. Select BROIL, set temperature to LO, and set time to 20 minutes.
6. Place the chicken breasts in the SearPlate. Open door and install the SearPlate in the bottom level of the unit. Close door and begin cooking.
7. When cooking is complete, carefully remove SearPlate from the oven. Enjoy!

Crispy Chicken Wings

PREP TIME: 15 minutes
COOK TIME: 20 minutes

nonstick spray
3 tbsps. vegetable oil
1 pound (454 g) chicken wings
½ cup all-purpose flour
½ tsp. smoked paprika
½ tsp. garlic powder

½ tsp. kosher salt
1½ tsps. freshly cracked black pepper

1. Place the chicken wings in a large bowl. Drizzle the vegetable oil over wings and toss to coat well.
2. In a separate bowl, whisk together the flour, paprika, garlic powder, salt, and pepper until combined.
3. Dredge the wings in the flour mixture one at a time, coating them well.
4. Remove Air Fry Basket from oven. Select AIR FRY, set temperature to 400°F, and set time to 22 minutes. Press the setting dial to begin preheating.
5. While unit is preheating, arrange wings in the basket, making sure they are not crowding each other. Spray with nonstick spray.
6. When unit has preheated, open door, install the SearPlate in the bottom level of the unit and the basket in the top level of the unit. Close door to begin cooking, until the breading is browned and crunchy, flipping halfway through cooking.
7. When cooking is complete, carefully remove basket from the oven. Serve hot.

Sweet and Salty Chicken Kebobs

PREP TIME: 20 minutes
COOK TIME: 12 minutes

cooking spay
4 (4-ounce) skinless, boneless chicken thighs, cubed into 1-inch size
¼ cup light soy sauce
5 scallions, cut into 1-inch pieces lengthwise
Wooden skewers, presoaked
1 tbsp. mirin
1 tsp. garlic salt
1 tsp. sugar

1. Mix the soy sauce, mirin, garlic salt and sugar in a large baking dish.
2. Thread the scallions and chicken cubes onto pre-soaked wooden skewers.
3. Coat the skewers generously with marinade. Spray with cooking spay.
4. Install SearPlate in the bottom level of the unit, then close the door. Select AIR ROAST, set temperature to 355°F, and set time to 12 minutes. Press the setting dial to begin preheating.
5. When unit has preheated, open door and use oven mitts to remove SearPlate and place it on top of oven. Transfer skewers to the SearPlate.
6. Reinstall the SearPlate in the bottom level of the unit. Close door to begin cooking, flipping halfway through cooking.
7. When cooking is complete, carefully remove SearPlate from oven with oven mitts. Serve warm.

Chicken and Mushroom Casserole

PREP TIME: 15 minutes
COOK TIME: 20 minutes

Cooking spray
4 chicken breasts
1 broccoli, cut into florets
1 cup mushrooms
½ cup shredded Parmesan cheese
1 tbsp. curry powder
1 cup coconut milk
Salt, to taste

1. Spritz a casserole dish with cooking spray.
2. Cube the chicken breasts and combine with curry powder and coconut milk in a medium bowl. Season with salt to taste.
3. Add the broccoli and mushroom and mix well.
4. Pour this mixture into the casserole dish. Top with the Parmesan cheese.
5. Install rack in bottom position, then close door. Select BAKE, set temperature to 350°F, and set time to 20 minutes. Press the setting dial to begin preheating.
6. When unit has preheated, open door and place casserole dish onto the center of the rack. Close door to begin cooking.
7. When cooking is complete, carefully remove the dish from the oven. Let cool for 5-10 minutes and serve warm.

Crispy Chicken Drumsticks

PREP TIME: 15 minutes
COOK TIME: 20 minutes

nonstick spray
4 (4-ounces) chicken drumsticks
½ cup panko breadcrumbs
½ cup buttermilk
½ cup all-purpose flour
¼ tsp. dried oregano
¼ tsp. baking powder
¼ tsp. dried thyme
¼ tsp. garlic powder
¼ tsp. ground ginger
¼ tsp. celery salt
¼ tsp. cayenne pepper
¼ tsp. paprika
Salt and ground black pepper, as required

1. Put the chicken drumsticks and buttermilk in a resealable plastic bag.
2. Seal the bag tightly and refrigerate for at least 3 hours.
3. Mix the flour, breadcrumbs, baking powder, herbs and spices in a small bowl.
4. Remove the chicken drumsticks from the bag and coat the chicken drumsticks evenly with the seasoned flour mixture.
5. Remove Air Fry Basket from oven. Select AIR FRY, set temperature to 400°F, and set time to 20 minutes. Press the setting dial to begin preheating.
6. While unit is preheating, arrange chicken drumsticks in the basket. Spray with nonstick spray.
7. When unit has preheated, open door, install the SearPlate in the bottom level of the unit and the basket in the top level of the unit. Close door to begin cooking, flipping halfway through cooking.
8. When cooking is complete, carefully remove basket from the oven. Serve hot.

Crispy Herbed Turkey Breast

PREP TIME: 5 minutes
COOK TIME: 25 minutes

½ tbsp. fresh rosemary, chopped
½ tbsp. fresh parsley, chopped
2 turkey breasts
1 garlic clove, minced
1 tbsp. ginger, minced
1 tsp. five spice powder
Salt and black pepper, to taste

1. Install SearPlate in the bottom level of the unit, then close door. Select SEAR CRISP, set temperature to 425°F, and set time to 25 minutes. Press the setting dial to begin preheating.
2. While unit is preheating, mix the garlic, herbs, five spice powder, salt and black pepper in a small bowl.
3. Brush the turkey breasts generously with garlic mixture.
4. When unit has preheated, open door, carefully remove the SearPlate with oven mitts and place on top of oven. Place the turkey breasts on the SearPlate.
5. Reinstall the SearPlate in the bottom level of the unit and close the door to begin cooking. After 25 minutes, begin to check turkey for doneness. If further doneness is desired, leave in oven.
6. When cooking is complete, remove the turkey breasts from the SearPlate. Serve warm.

Sweet and Sour Chicken Thighs

PREP TIME: 15 minutes
COOK TIME: 18 minutes

nonstick spray
2 (4-ounces) skinless, boneless chicken thighs
½ cup corn flour
1 garlic clove, minced
1 scallion, finely chopped
1 tsp. sugar
½ tbsp. soy sauce
½ tbsp. rice vinegar
Salt and black pepper, as required

1. Mix all the ingredients except the chicken thighs and corn flour in a bowl.
2. Place the corn flour in another bowl.
3. Coat the chicken thighs into the marinade and then dredge into the corn flour.
4. Remove Air Fry Basket from oven. Select AIR FRY, set temperature to 390°F, and set time to 18 minutes. Press the setting dial to begin preheating.
5. While unit is preheating, arrange chicken thighs in the basket, skin side down. Spray with nonstick spray.
6. When unit has preheated, open door, install the SearPlate in the bottom level of the unit and the basket in the top level of the unit. Close door to begin cooking, flipping halfway through cooking.
7. When cooking is complete, carefully remove basket from the oven. Serve hot.

Piri-Piri Chicken Thighs

PREP TIME: 5 minutes
COOK TIME: 25 minutes

¼ cup piri-piri sauce
1 tbsp. freshly squeezed lemon juice
2 tbsps. brown sugar, divided
2 cloves garlic, minced
1 tbsp. canola oil
4 bone-in, skin-on chicken thighs, each weighing approximately 7 to 8 ounces (198 to 227 g)
½ tsp. cornstarch

1. To make the marinade, whisk together the lemon juice, piri-piri sauce, 1 tbsp. of brown sugar, and the garlic in a small bowl. While whisking, gently pour in the oil in a steady stream and continue to whisk until emulsified.
2. Using a skewer, poke holes in the chicken thighs and place them in a small glass dish. Pour the marinade over the chicken and turn the thighs to coat them with the sauce. Cover the dish and refrigerate for at least 15 minutes and up to 1 hour.
3. Install SearPlate in the bottom level of the unit, then close the door. Select AIR ROAST, set temperature to 400°F, and set time to 25 minutes. Press the setting dial to begin preheating.
4. When unit has preheated, open door and use oven mitts to remove SearPlate and place it on top of oven. Remove the chicken thighs from the dish, reserving the marinade, and place them skin-side down to the SearPlate.
5. Reinstall the SearPlate in the bottom level of the unit. Close door to begin cooking.
6. Meanwhile, whisk the remaining brown sugar and the cornstarch into the marinade and microwave it on high power for 1 minute until it is bubbling and thickened to a glaze.
7. When the chicken has cooked for 20 minutes, open door, turn the thighs over and brush them with the glaze. Close door to finish cooking, until the glaze browns and begins to char in spots.
8. When cooking is complete, carefully remove SearPlate from oven with oven mitts. Transfer the chicken to a platter and serve with additional piri-piri sauce, if desired.

Appetizing Chicken

PREP TIME: 30 minutes
COOK TIME: 16 minutes

¾ pound chicken pieces
1 tbsp. fresh rosemary, chopped
1 lemon, cut into wedges
1 tsp. ginger, minced
1 tbsp. soy sauce
½ tbsp. canola oil
1 tbsp. oyster sauce
3 tbsps. coconut sugar

1. Mix chicken, ginger, soy sauce and canola oil in a medium bowl.
2. Marinate and refrigerate for about 30 minutes.
3. Install SearPlate in the bottom level of the unit, then close the door. Select AIR ROAST, set temperature to 400°F, and set time to 18 minutes. Press the setting dial to begin preheating.
4. When unit has preheated, open door and use oven mitts to remove SearPlate and place it on top of oven. Transfer chicken to the SearPlate.
5. Reinstall the SearPlate in the bottom level of the unit. Close door to begin cooking.
6. After 6 minutes, open door and mix the remaining ingredients in a small bowl to spread over the chicken. Squeeze juice from lemon wedges over chicken and top with the wedges. Close door to finish cooking.
7. When cooking is complete, carefully remove SearPlate from oven with oven mitts. Serve warm.

CHAPTER 6

VEGETABLES

Roasted Asparagus and Mashed Potato

PREP TIME: 5 minutes
COOK TIME: 25 minutes

4 medium potatoes
1 bunch asparagus
⅓ cup cottage cheese
⅓ cup low-fat crème fraiche
1 tbsp. wholegrain mustard
Salt and pepper, to taste

1. Install SearPlate in the bottom level of the unit, then close the door. Select AIR ROAST, set temperature to 400°F, and set time to 25 minutes. Press the setting dial to begin preheating.
2. When unit has preheated, open door and use oven mitts to remove SearPlate and place it on top of oven. Transfer potatoes to the SearPlate.
3. Reinstall the SearPlate in the bottom level of the unit. Close door to begin cooking.
4. After 12 minutes, open door and place the asparagus on the SearPlate. Close door to finish cooking.
5. When cooking is complete, carefully remove SearPlate from oven with oven mitts.
6. Remove the potatoes and mash them with rest of ingredients. Sprinkle with salt and pepper to taste. Serve the mash with Asparagus.

Air Fried Brussels Sprouts

PREP TIME: 5 minutes
COOK TIME: 12 minutes

nonstick spray
1 tbsp. coconut oil, melted
1 pound (454 g) Brussels sprouts, halved
1 tbsp. unsalted butter, melted

1. Remove Air Fry Basket from oven. Select AIR FRY, set temperature to 400°F, and set time to 12 minutes. Press the setting dial to begin preheating.
2. While unit is preheating, combine the Brussels sprouts with the melted coconut oil.
3. Arrange Brussels sprouts in the basket, making sure they are not crowding each other. Spray with nonstick spray.
4. When unit has preheated, open door, install the SearPlate in the bottom level of the unit and the basket in the top level of the unit. Close door to begin cooking, shaking halfway through cooking.
5. When cooking is complete, carefully remove basket from the oven. Serve with a topping of melted butter.

Easy Roasted Asparagus

PREP TIME: 5 minutes
COOK TIME: 8 minutes

1 tsp. canola oil
1 pound (454 g) asparagus, trimmed
and halved crosswise
Salt and pepper, to taste
Lemon wedges, for serving

1. Install SearPlate in the bottom level of the unit, then close the door. Select AIR ROAST, set temperature to 400°F, and set time to 8 minutes. Press the setting dial to begin preheating.
2. Toss the asparagus with the oil, ⅛ tsp. salt, and ⅛ tsp. pepper in a medium bowl.
3. When unit has preheated, open door and use oven mitts to remove SearPlate and place it on top of oven. Transfer asparagus to the SearPlate.
4. Reinstall the SearPlate in the bottom level of the unit. Close door to begin cooking, until tender and bright green, flipping halfway through cooking.
5. When cooking is complete, carefully remove SearPlate from oven with oven mitts. Season with salt and pepper and serve with lemon wedges.

Air Fried Green Tomatoes

PREP TIME: 5 minutes
COOK TIME: 16 minutes

nonstick spray
4 medium green tomatoes
1 cup ground almonds
½ cup panko bread crumbs
⅓ cup all purpose flour
2 egg whites
¼ cup almond milk
2 tsps. canola oil
1 tsp. paprika
1 clove garlic, minced

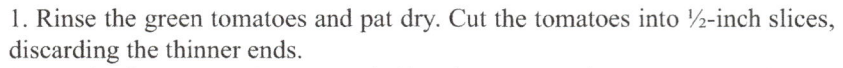

1. Rinse the green tomatoes and pat dry. Cut the tomatoes into ½-inch slices, discarding the thinner ends.
2. Put the flour on a plate. In a shallow bowl, beat the egg whites with the almond milk until frothy. In another plate, combine the canola oil, almonds, bread crumbs, paprika and garlic and mix well.
3. Dip the tomato slices into the flour, then into the egg white mixture, then into the almond mixture to coat.
4. Remove Air Fry Basket from oven. Select AIR FRY, set temperature to 400°F, and set time to 8 minutes. Press the setting dial to begin preheating.
5. While unit is preheating, arrange half of tomato slices in the basket, making sure they are not crowding each other. Spray with nonstick spray.
6. When unit has preheated, open door, install the SearPlate in the bottom level of the unit and the basket in the top level of the unit. Close door to begin cooking, until the tomato coating is crisp and golden brown.
7. Repeat with the remaining tomato slices.
8. When cooking is complete, carefully remove basket from the oven. Serve immediately.

Eggplant and Rice Bowl

PREP TIME: 15 minutes
COOK TIME: 10 minutes

¼ cup sliced cucumber
1 tsp. salt
1 tbsp. sugar
7 tbsps. Japanese rice vinegar
3 medium eggplants, sliced

3 tbsps. sweet white miso paste
1 tbsp. mirin rice wine
4 cups cooked sushi rice
4 spring onions
1 tbsp. toasted sesame seeds

1. Coat the cucumber slices with the rice wine vinegar, salt, and sugar.
2. Put a dish on top of the bowl to weight it down completely.
3. In a bowl, mix the eggplants, mirin rice wine and miso paste. Allow to marinate for 30 minutes.
4. Install SearPlate in the bottom level of the unit, then close the door. Select AIR ROAST, set temperature to 400°F, and set time to 10 minutes. Press the setting dial to begin preheating.
5. When unit has preheated, open door and use oven mitts to remove SearPlate and place it on top of oven. Transfer the eggplant slices to the SearPlate.
6. Reinstall the SearPlate in the bottom level of the unit. Close door to begin cooking, flipping halfway through cooking.
7. When cooking is complete, carefully remove SearPlate from oven with oven mitts. Fill the bottom of a serving bowl with rice and top with the eggplants and pickled cucumbers.
8. Garnish with the spring onions and sesame seeds. Serve immediately.

Breadcrumbs Stuffed Mushrooms

PREP TIME: 15 minutes
COOK TIME: 10 minutes

nonstick spray
16 small button mushrooms, stemmed and gills removed
1½ spelt bread slices
1 tbsp. flat-leaf parsley, finely chopped
1½ tbsps. canola oil
1 garlic clove, crushed
Salt and black pepper, to taste

1. Put the bread slices in a food processor and pulse until fine crumbs form.
2. Transfer the crumbs into a small bowl and stir in the canola oil, garlic, parsley, salt, and black pepper.
3. Stuff the breadcrumbs mixture in each mushroom cap.
4. Remove Air Fry Basket from oven. Select AIR FRY, set temperature to 390°F, and set time to 10 minutes. Press the setting dial to begin preheating.
5. While unit is preheating, arrange mushrooms in the basket, making sure they are not crowding each other. Spray with nonstick spray.
6. When unit has preheated, open door, install the SearPlate in the bottom level of the unit and the basket in the top level of the unit. Close door to begin cooking.
7. When cooking is complete, carefully remove basket from the oven. Transfer to a serving bowl and serve warm.

Sweet and Spicy Parsnips

PREP TIME: 15 minutes
COOK TIME: 35 minutes

1 tbsp. canola
2 pounds parsnip, peeled and cut into 1-inch chunks
2 tbsps. honey
1 tbsp. dried parsley flakes, crushed
¼ tsp. red pepper flakes, crushed
Salt and ground black pepper, to taste

1. Install SearPlate in the bottom level of the unit, then close the door. Select AIR ROAST, set temperature to 400°F, and set time to 35 minutes. Press the setting dial to begin preheating.
2. Mix the parsnips and canola oil in a large bowl and toss to coat well.
3. When unit has preheated, open door and use oven mitts to remove SearPlate and place it on top of oven. Transfer parsnip chunks to the SearPlate.
4. Reinstall the SearPlate in the bottom level of the unit. Close door to begin cooking.
5. After 30 minutes, mix the remaining ingredients in another large bowl. Open door and stir in the parsnip chunks. Arrange the parsnip chunks on the SearPlate. Close door to finish cooking.
6. When cooking is complete, carefully remove SearPlate from oven with oven mitts. Transfer the parsnip chunks onto serving plates and serve hot.

Sesame Seeds Bok Choy

Serves 4

PREP TIME: 10 minutes
COOK TIME: 6 minutes

nonstick spray
4 bunches baby bok choy, bottoms removed and leaves separated
1 tsp. sesame seeds
1 tsp. garlic powder

1. Remove Air Fry Basket from oven. Select AIR FRY, set temperature to 325°F, and set time to 6 minutes. Press the setting dial to begin preheating.
2. While unit is preheating, arrange bok choy leaves in the basket. Sprinkle with garlic powder and spray with nonstick spray.
3. When unit has preheated, open door, install the SearPlate in the bottom level of the unit and the basket in the top level of the unit. Close door to begin cooking, shaking twice in between.
4. When cooking is complete, carefully remove basket from the oven. Transfer the bok choy onto serving plates and serve garnished with sesame seeds.

Roasted Mushrooms with Peas

PREP TIME: 15 minutes
COOK TIME: 16 minutes

16 ounces cremini mushrooms, halved
½ cup frozen peas
4 garlic cloves, finely chopped
½ cup soy sauce
4 tbsps. maple syrup
4 tbsps. rice vinegar
2 tsps. Chinese five spice powder
½ tsp. ground ginger

1. Install SearPlate in the bottom level of the unit, then close the door. Select AIR ROAST, set temperature to 400°F, and set time to 16 minutes. Press the setting dial to begin preheating.
2. While unit is preheating, mix the soy sauce, maple syrup, vinegar, garlic, five spice powder, and ground ginger in a small bowl.
3. When unit has preheated, open door and use oven mitts to remove SearPlate and place it on top of oven. Transfer mushrooms to the SearPlate.
4. Reinstall the SearPlate in the bottom level of the unit. Close door to begin cooking.
5. After 10 minutes, open door and stir in the soy sauce mixture and peas. Close door to finish cooking.
6. When cooking is complete, carefully remove SearPlate from oven with oven mitts. Transfer the mushroom mixture in plates and serve hot.

Tofu with Veggies

Serves 3

PREP TIME: 25 minutes
COOK TIME: 20 minutes

½ (14-ounces) block firm tofu, pressed and crumbled
1 cup carrot, peeled and chopped
3 cups cauliflower rice
½ cup broccoli, finely chopped
½ cup frozen peas
4 tbsps. low-sodium soy sauce, divided
2 garlic cloves, minced
1 tbsp. fresh ginger, minced

1 tbsp. rice vinegar
1 tsp. ground turmeric
1½ tsps. sesame oil, toasted

1. Install SearPlate in the bottom level of the unit, then close door. Select SEAR CRISP, set temperature to 400°F, and set time to 20 minutes. Press the setting dial to begin preheating.
2. While unit is preheating, mix the tofu, carrot, onion, 2 tbsps. of soy sauce, and turmeric in a medium bowl.
3. When unit has preheated, open door, carefully remove the SearPlate with oven mitts and place on top of oven. Place the tofu mixture on the SearPlate.
4. Reinstall the SearPlate in the bottom level of the unit and close the door to begin cooking.
5. Meanwhile, combine the cauliflower rice, broccoli, peas, garlic, ginger, vinegar, sesame oil, and remaining soy sauce in a large bowl.
6. After 10 minutes, open door and stir in the cauliflower mixture. Close door to finish cooking.
7. When cooking is complete, remove the tofu mixture from the SearPlate and serve hot.

CHAPTER 7

PORK

Bacon Wrapped Pork Tenderloin

PREP TIME: 15 minutes
COOK TIME: 20 minutes

1 (1½ pounds) pork tenderloin
4 bacon strips
2 tbsps. Dijon mustard

1. Install SearPlate in the bottom level of the unit, then close door. Select SEAR CRISP, set temperature to 425°F, and set time to 20 minutes. Press the setting dial to begin preheating.
2. While unit is preheating, rub the tenderloin evenly with mustard and wrap the tenderloin with bacon strips.
3. When unit has preheated, open door, carefully remove the SearPlate with oven mitts and place on top of oven. Place the pork tenderloin on the SearPlate.
4. Reinstall the SearPlate in the bottom level of the unit and close the door to begin cooking, flipping once in between.
5. When cooking is complete, make sure pork is cooked through with a thermometer. The internal temperature should read 145°F or higher.
6. Let the pork tenderloin rest for 5 minutes, then cut into desired size slices to serve.

Pork Loin with Potatoes

Serves 5

PREP TIME: 15 minutes
COOK TIME: 20 minutes

3 tbsps. canola oil, divided
2 pounds pork loin
3 large red potatoes, chopped
1 tsp. fresh parsley, chopped
Salt and ground black pepper, as required

½ tsp. garlic powder
½ tsp. red pepper flakes, crushed

1. Install SearPlate in the bottom level of the unit, then close door. Select SEAR CRISP, set temperature to 425°F, and set time to 20 minutes. Press the setting dial to begin preheating.
2. While unit is preheating, rub the pork loin evenly with 1½ tbsps. canola oil, parsley, salt, and black pepper.
3. Mix the red potatoes, remaining oil, garlic powder, red pepper flakes, salt, and black pepper in a medium bowl.
4. When unit has preheated, open door, carefully remove the SearPlate with oven mitts and place on top of oven. Place the pork loin on the left side and potatoes on the right.
5. Reinstall the SearPlate in the bottom level of the unit and close the door to begin cooking.
6. When cooking is complete, make sure pork is cooked through with a thermometer. The internal temperature should read 145°F or higher.
7. Remove the potatoes and pork from the SearPlate. Cut the pork into your desired size slices and serve alongside potatoes.

Barbecue Pork Ribs

PREP TIME: 5 minutes
COOK TIME: 25 minutes

1 tsp. sesame oil
1 pound (454 g) pork ribs, chopped
1 tbsp. barbecue dry rub
1 tsp. mustard
1 tbsp. apple cider vinegar

1. Combine the dry rub, mustard, apple cider vinegar, and sesame oil in a medium bowl, then coat the ribs with this mixture. Refrigerate the ribs for 20 minutes.
2. Install SearPlate in the bottom level of the unit, then close the door. Select AIR ROAST, set temperature to 400°F, and set time to 25 minutes. Press the setting dial to begin preheating.
3. When unit has preheated, open door and use oven mitts to remove SearPlate and place it on top of oven. Transfer ribs to the SearPlate.
4. Reinstall the SearPlate in the bottom level of the unit. Close door to begin cooking, flipping halfway through cooking.
5. When cooking is complete, carefully remove SearPlate from oven with oven mitts. Serve immediately.

BBQ Pork Steaks

Serves 4

PREP TIME: 5 minutes
COOK TIME: 12 minutes

4 pork steaks
½ cup brown sugar
½ cup ketchup
1 tbsp. Cajun seasoning
2 tbsps. BBQ sauce
1 tbsp. vinegar
1 tsp. soy sauce

1. Install SearPlate in the bottom level of the unit, then close door. Select SEAR CRISP, set temperature to 400°F, and set time to 12 minutes. Press the setting dial to begin preheating.
2. While unit is preheating, Sprinkle the pork steaks with Cajun seasoning. Combine the remaining ingredients and brush onto the steaks.
3. When unit has preheated, open door, carefully remove the SearPlate with oven mitts and place on top of oven. Place the pork steaks on the SearPlate.
4. Reinstall the SearPlate in the bottom level of the unit and close the door to begin cooking.
5. When cooking is complete, make sure pork is cooked through with a thermometer. The internal temperature should read 145°F or higher.
6. Remove the pork steaks from the SearPlate and serve immediately.

Mexican Pork Chops

PREP TIME: 5 minutes
COOK TIME: 15 minutes

1 tbsp. canola oil
2 (4-ounce / 113-g) boneless pork chops
¼ tsp. dried oregano
1½ tsps. taco seasoning mix
1 tbsp. unsalted butter

1. Install SearPlate in the bottom level of the unit, then close door. Select SEAR CRISP, set temperature to 400°F, and set time to 15 minutes. Press the setting dial to begin preheating.
2. While unit is preheating, combine the dried oregano and taco seasoning in a small bowl and rub the mixture into the pork chops. Brush the chops with 1 tbsp. canola oil.
3. When unit has preheated, open door, carefully remove the SearPlate with oven mitts and place on top of oven. Place the pork chops on the SearPlate.
4. Reinstall the SearPlate in the bottom level of the unit and close the door to begin cooking.
5. When cooking is complete, make sure pork is cooked through with a thermometer. The internal temperature should read 145°F. Remove the pork chops from the SearPlate. Serve with a garnish of butter.

Baked Chorizo Scotch Eggs

Makes 4 eggs

PREP TIME: 5 minutes
COOK TIME: 18 minutes

Cooking spray
1 pound (454 g) Mexican chorizo or other seasoned sausage meat
4 soft-boiled eggs plus 1 raw egg
1 cup panko bread crumbs
1 tbsp. water
½ cup all-purpose flour

1. Divide the chorizo into 4 equal portions. Flatten each portion into a disc. Place a soft-boiled egg in the center of each disc. Wrap the chorizo around the egg, encasing it completely. Place the encased eggs on a plate and chill for at least 30 minutes.
2. Beat the raw egg with 1 tbsp. water. Put the flour on a small plate and the panko on a second plate.
3. Working with 1 egg at a time, roll the encased egg in the flour, then dip it in the egg mixture. Dredge the egg in the panko and arrange on a plate. Repeat with the remaining eggs. Spray the eggs with cooking spray.
4. Install SearPlate in the bottom level of the unit, then close the door. Select BAKE, set temperature to 360°F, and set time to 18 minutes. Press the setting dial to begin preheating.
5. When unit has preheated, open door and use oven mitts to remove SearPlate and place it on top of oven. Transfer eggs to the SearPlate.
6. Reinstall the SearPlate in the bottom level of the unit. Close door to begin cooking, until browned and crisp on all sides.
7. When cooking is complete, carefully remove SearPlate from oven with oven mitts. Serve immediately.

Easy Devils on Horseback

Serves 12

PREP TIME: 5 minutes
COOK TIME: 14 minutes

nonstick spray
24 petite pitted prunes (4½ ounces / 128 g)
8 slices center-cut bacon, cut crosswise into thirds
¼ cup crumbled blue cheese, divided

1. Halve the prunes lengthwise, but don't cut them all the way through. Place ½ tsp. of cheese in the center of each prune. Wrap a piece of bacon around each prune and secure the bacon with a toothpick.
2. Remove Air Fry Basket from oven. Select AIR FRY, set temperature to 400°F, and set time to 7 minutes. Press the setting dial to begin preheating.
3. While unit is preheating, arrange half of the prunes in the basket, making sure they are not crowding each other. Spray with nonstick spray.
4. When unit has preheated, open door, install the SearPlate in the bottom level of the unit and the basket in the top level of the unit. Close door to begin cooking until the bacon is cooked through and crisp, flipping halfway through cooking.
5. Repeat with the remaining prunes.
6. When cooking is complete, carefully remove basket from the oven. Let cool slightly and serve warm.

Citrus Pork Loin

Serves 8

PREP TIME: 10 minutes
COOK TIME: 28 minutes

Cooking spray
2 pound (907 g) boneless pork loin roast
1 tbsp. lime juice
1 tbsp. orange marmalade
1 tsp. coarse brown mustard
1 tsp. curry powder
1 tsp. dried lemongrass
Salt and ground black pepper, to taste

1. Mix the lime juice, marmalade, mustard, curry powder, and lemongrass.
2. Rub mixture all over the surface of the pork loin. Season with salt and pepper.
3. Install SearPlate in the bottom level of the unit, then close the door. Select AIR ROAST, set temperature to 425°F, and set time to 28 minutes. Press the setting dial to begin preheating.
4. When unit has preheated, open door and use oven mitts to remove SearPlate and place it on top of oven. Transfer pork roast diagonally to the SearPlate and spray with cooking spray.
5. Reinstall the SearPlate in the bottom level of the unit. Close door to begin cooking, flipping halfway through cooking.
6. When cooking is complete, make sure pork is cooked through with a thermometer. The internal temperature should read 145°F or higher.
7. Remove SearPlate from oven with oven mitts. Wrap roast in foil and let rest for 10 minutes before slicing. Serve immediately.

Five Spice Pork Belly

PREP TIME: 15 minutes
COOK TIME: 20 minutes

nonstick spray
1-pound pork belly
2 tbsps. swerve
2 tbsps. dark soy sauce
1 tbsp. hoisin sauce
1 tbsp. Shaoxing (cooking wine)
2 tsps. garlic, minced

2 tsps. ginger, minced
1 tsp. Chinese Five Spice

1. Mix all the ingredients in a bowl and place in the Ziplock bag.
2. Seal the bag, shake it well and refrigerate to marinate for about 1 hour.
3. Remove Air Fry Basket from oven. Select AIR FRY, set temperature to 390°F, and set time to 15 minutes. Press the setting dial to begin preheating.
4. While unit is preheating, remove the pork from the bag and arrange in the basket. Spray with nonstick spray.
5. When unit has preheated, open door, install the SearPlate in the bottom level of the unit and the basket in the top level of the unit. Close door to begin cooking, flipping halfway through cooking.
6. When cooking is complete, carefully remove basket from the oven. Serve warm.

Glazed Ham

Serves 4

PREP TIME: 10 minutes
COOK TIME: 40 minutes

1 pound (10½ ounce) ham joint
¾ cup whiskey
2 tbsps. honey
2 tbsps. French mustard

1. Mix all the ingredients in a small bowl except the ham.
2. Keep the ham joint for about 30 minutes at room temperature.
3. Install SearPlate in the bottom level of the unit, then close the door. Select AIR ROAST, set temperature to 325°F, and set time to 40 minutes. Press the setting dial to begin preheating.
4. When unit has preheated, open door and use oven mitts to remove SearPlate and place it on top of oven. Transfer the ham to the SearPlate and top with half of the whiskey mixture.
5. Reinstall the SearPlate in the bottom level of the unit. Close door to begin cooking.
6. After 4 minutes, open door and coat the ham with the remaining whiskey mixture. Close door to finish cooking.
7. When cooking is complete, carefully remove SearPlate from oven with oven mitts. Transfer to a platter and serve warm.

CHAPTER 8

LAMB

Leg of Lamb with Brussels Sprouts

Serves 6

PREP TIME: 20 minutes
COOK TIME: 60 minutes

2¼ pounds leg of lamb
1 tbsp. fresh rosemary, minced
1 tbsp. fresh lemon thyme
1½ pounds Brussels sprouts, trimmed
3 tbsps. canola oil, divided

1 garlic clove, minced
Salt and ground black pepper, as required
2 tbsps. honey

1. Make slits in the leg of lamb with a sharp knife.
2. Mix 2 tbsps. of oil, herbs, garlic, salt, and black pepper in a bowl.
3. Coat the leg of lamb with oil mixture generously.
4. Install SearPlate in the bottom level of the unit, then close the door. Select AIR ROAST, set temperature to 400°F, and set time to 60 minutes. Press the setting dial to begin preheating.
5. When unit has preheated, open door and use oven mitts to remove SearPlate and place it on top of oven. Transfer the lamb leg to the SearPlate.
6. Reinstall the SearPlate in the bottom level of the unit. Close door to begin cooking.
7. Meanwhile, coat the Brussels sprouts evenly with the remaining oil and honey in another medium bowl.
8. After 50 minutes, open door and arrange the Brussels sprouts on the SearPlate. Close the door to finish cooking.
9. When cooking is complete, carefully remove SearPlate from oven with oven mitts. Transfer the lamb and Brussels sprouts to a plate and serve warm.

Simple Lamb Chops

Serves 2

PREP TIME: 10 minutes
COOK TIME: 12 minutes

1 tbsp. vegetable oil
4 (4-ounces) lamb chops
Salt and black pepper, to taste

1. Install SearPlate in the bottom level of the unit, then close door. Select SEAR CRISP, set temperature to 400°F, and set time to 12 minutes. Press the setting dial to begin preheating.
2. While unit is preheating, mix the vegetable oil, salt, and black pepper in a large bowl and add the chops.
3. When unit has preheated, open door, carefully remove the SearPlate with oven mitts and place on top of oven. Place the chops on the SearPlate.
4. Reinstall the SearPlate in the bottom level of the unit and close the door to begin cooking, flipping halfway through cooking.
5. When cooking is complete, make sure lamb is cooked through with a thermometer. The internal temperature should read 145°F. Transfer the lamb chops to a plate and serve hot.

Lamb Ribs with Mint Yogurt

PREP TIME: 5 minutes
COOK TIME: 18 minutes

nonstick spray
2 tbsps. mustard
1 pound (454 g) lamb ribs
1 tsp. rosemary, chopped
¼ cup mint leaves, chopped
1 cup Greek yogurt
Salt and ground black pepper, to taste

1. Remove Air Fry Basket from oven. Select AIR FRY, set temperature to 350°F, and set time to 18 minutes. Press the setting dial to begin preheating.
2. While unit is preheating, use a brush to apply the mustard to the lamb ribs, and season with rosemary, salt and pepper to taste.
3. Arrange lamb ribs in the basket, making sure they are not crowding each other. Spray with nonstick spray.
4. When unit has preheated, open door, install the SearPlate in the bottom level of the unit and the basket in the top level of the unit. Close door to begin cooking, flipping halfway through cooking.
5. Meanwhile, combine the mint leaves and yogurt in a bowl.
6. When cooking is complete, carefully remove basket from the oven. Serve the lambn ribs with the mint yogurt.

Spicy Lamb Satay

PREP TIME: 5 minutes
COOK TIME: 8 minutes

Cooking spray
2 boneless lamb steaks
¼ tsp. cumin
1 tsp. ginger
½ tsp. nutmeg
Salt and ground black pepper, to taste

1. Combine the cumin, ginger, nutmeg, salt and pepper in a medium bowl.
2. Cube the lamb steaks and massage the spice mixture into each one.
3. Leave to marinate for about 10 minutes, then transfer onto metal skewers.
4. Install SearPlate in the bottom level of the unit, then close the door. Select AIR ROAST, set temperature to 400°F, and set time to 8 minutes. Press the setting dial to begin preheating.
5. When unit has preheated, open door and use oven mitts to remove SearPlate and place it on top of oven. Transfer skewers to the SearPlate and spray with the cooking spray.
6. Reinstall the SearPlate in the bottom level of the unit. Close door to begin cooking, flipping halfway through cooking.
7. When cooking is complete, carefully remove SearPlate from oven with oven mitts. Serve hot.

Lamb Meatballs

PREP TIME: 20 minutes
COOK TIME: 23 minutes

For the Meatballs:
nonstick spray
½ small onion, finely diced
1 clove garlic, minced
1 pound (454 g) ground lamb
2 tbsps. fresh parsley, finely chopped (plus more for garnish)
2 tsps. fresh oregano, finely chopped
2 tbsps. milk
1 egg yolk
Salt and freshly ground black pepper, to taste

½ cup crumbled feta cheese, for garnish
For the Tomato Sauce:
2 tbsps. butter
1 clove garlic, smashed
Pinch crushed red pepper flakes
¼ tsp. ground cinnamon
1 (28-ounce / 794-g) can crushed tomatoes
Salt, to taste

1. Combine all the meatballs ingredients in a large bowl and mix just until everything is combined. Shape the mixture into 1½-inch balls or shape the meat between two spoons to make quenelles.
2. Make the tomato sauce: Put the butter, garlic and red pepper flakes in a sauté pan and heat over medium heat on the stovetop. Let the garlic sizzle a little, but before the butter browns, add the cinnamon and tomatoes. Bring to a simmer and simmer for 15 minutes. Season with salt to taste.
3. Remove Air Fry Basket from oven. Select AIR FRY, set temperature to 400°F, and set time to 8 minutes. Press the setting dial to begin preheating.
4. While unit is preheating, arrange the meatballs in the basket, making sure they are not crowding each other. Spray with nonstick spray.
5. When unit has preheated, open door, install the SearPlate in the bottom level of the unit and the basket in the top level of the unit. Close door to begin cooking, shaking halfway through cooking.
6. When cooking is complete, carefully remove basket from the oven. To serve, spoon a pool of the tomato sauce onto plates and place the meatballs. Top with the feta cheese and garnish with more fresh parsley. Serve immediately.

Roasted Lamb

PREP TIME: 15 minutes
COOK TIME: 1 hour

1 tbsp. canola oil
2½ pounds half lamb leg roast, slits carved
2 garlic cloves, sliced into smaller slithers
1 tbsp. dried rosemary
Cracked Himalayan rock salt and cracked peppercorns, to taste

1. Install SearPlate in the bottom level of the unit, then close the door. Select AIR ROAST, set temperature to 400°F, and set time to 60 minutes. Press the setting dial to begin preheating.
2. While unit is preheating, insert the garlic slithers in the slits of lamb and brush with rosemary, oil, salt and black pepper.
3. When unit has preheated, open door and use oven mitts to remove SearPlate and place it on top of oven. Transfer lamb to the SearPlate.
4. Reinstall the SearPlate in the bottom level of the unit. Close door to begin cooking, flipping halfway through cooking.
5. When cooking is complete, carefully remove SearPlate from oven with oven mitts. Serve hot.

Pesto Coated Rack of Lamb

PREP TIME: 15 minutes
COOK TIME: 15 minutes

¼ cup extra-virgin canola oil
1 (1½-pounds) rack of lamb
½ bunch fresh mint
1 garlic clove
½ tbsp. honey
Salt and black pepper, to taste

1. Put the garlic, mint, oil, honey, salt and black pepper in a blender and pulse until smooth to make pesto.
2. Coat the rack of lamb with this pesto on both sides.
3. Install SearPlate in the bottom level of the unit, then close the door. Select AIR ROAST, set temperature to 390°F, and set time to 15 minutes. Press the setting dial to begin preheating.
4. When unit has preheated, open door and use oven mitts to remove SearPlate and place it on top of oven. Transfer rack of lamb to the SearPlate.
5. Reinstall the SearPlate in the bottom level of the unit. Close door to begin cooking, flipping halfway through cooking.
6. After 15 minutes, begin to check lamb for doneness. If further doneness is desired, leave in oven.
7. When cooking is complete, carefully remove SearPlate from oven with oven mitts. Cut the rack into individual chops to serve.

Greek Lamb Rack

PREP TIME: 5 minutes
COOK TIME: 12 minutes

2 to 4 tbsps. canola oil
1 lamb rib rack (7 to 8 ribs)
¼ cup freshly squeezed lemon juice
1 tsp. oregano
2 tsps. minced fresh rosemary
1 tsp. minced fresh thyme
2 tbsps. minced garlic

Salt and freshly ground black pepper, to taste

1. In a small mixing bowl, combine the lemon juice, rosemary, thyme, oregano, garlic, salt, pepper, and canola oil and mix well.
2. Rub the mixture over the lamb, covering all the meat.
3. Install SearPlate in the bottom level of the unit, then close the door. Select AIR ROAST, set temperature to 390°F, and set time to 12 minutes. Press the setting dial to begin preheating.
4. When unit has preheated, open door and use oven mitts to remove SearPlate and place it on top of oven. Transfer the lamb to the SearPlate.
5. Reinstall the SearPlate in the bottom level of the unit. Close door to begin cooking, flipping halfway through cooking.
6. When cooking is complete, make sure lamb is cooked through with a thermometer. The internal temperature should read 145°F or higher.
7. Remove SearPlate from oven with oven mitts. Serve immediately.

Mustard Lamb Loin Chops

PREP TIME: 15 minutes
COOK TIME: 16 minutes

8 (4-ounces) lamb loin chops
2 tbsps. Dijon mustard
1 tbsp. fresh lemon juice
½ tsp. canola oil
1 tsp. dried tarragon
Salt and black pepper, to taste

1. Install SearPlate in the bottom level of the unit, then close door. Select SEAR CRISP, set temperature to 390°F, and set time to 16 minutes. Press the setting dial to begin preheating.
2. While unit is preheating, mix the mustard, lemon juice, oil, tarragon, salt, and black pepper in a large bowl.
3. Coat the chops generously with the mustard mixture.
4. When unit has preheated, open door, carefully remove the SearPlate with oven mitts and place on top of oven. Place the chops on the SearPlate.
5. Reinstall the SearPlate in the bottom level of the unit and close the door to begin cooking, flipping once in between.
6. When cooking is complete, make sure lamb is cooked through with a thermometer. The internal temperature should read 145°F. Remove the chops from the SearPlate and serve hot.

Spiced Lamb Steaks

Serves 3

PREP TIME: 15 minutes
COOK TIME: 15 minutes

cooking spray
1½ pounds boneless lamb sirloin steaks
½ onion, roughly chopped
5 garlic cloves, peeled
1 tbsp. fresh ginger, peeled
1 tsp. ground fennel
1 tsp. garam masala

½ tsp. ground cinnamon
½ tsp. ground cumin
½ tsp. cayenne pepper
Salt and black pepper, to taste

1. Put the garlic, ginger, onion, and spices in a blender and pulse until smooth.
2. Coat the lamb steaks with this mixture on both sides and refrigerate to marinate for about 24 hours.
3. Install SearPlate in the bottom level of the unit, then close door. Select SEAR CRISP, set temperature to 375°F, and set time to 15 minutes. Press the setting dial to begin preheating.
4. When unit has preheated, open door, carefully remove the SearPlate with oven mitts and place on top of oven. Place the lamb steaks on the SearPlate and spray with cooking spray.
5. Reinstall the SearPlate in the bottom level of the unit and close the door to begin cooking, flipping once in between.
6. When cooking is complete, remove the steaks from the SearPlate and serve warm.

CHAPTER 9

SNACK

Easy Crispy Prawns

PREP TIME: 15 minutes
COOK TIME: 8 minutes

nonstick spray
1 egg
½ pound nacho chips, crushed
18 prawns, peeled and deveined
Salt and black pepper, to taste

1. Crack the egg in a shallow dish and beat well.
2. Place the crushed nacho chips in another shallow dish.
3. Coat prawns with egg, salt and black pepper, then roll into nacho chips. Spray with cooking spray.
4. Remove Air Fry Basket from oven. Select AIR FRY, set temperature to 390°F, and set time to 8 minutes. Press the setting dial to begin preheating.
5. While unit is preheating, arrange prawns in the basket, making sure they are not crowding each other. Spray with nonstick spray.
6. When unit has preheated, open door, install the SearPlate in the bottom level of the unit and the basket in the top level of the unit. Close door to begin cooking, flipping once in between.
7. When cooking is complete, carefully remove basket from the oven. Serve warm.

Banana Chips

PREP TIME: 10 minutes
COOK TIME: 8 hours

spray bottle of lemon juice
2 medium bananas, peeled and cut across into ⅛-inch-thick slices

1. Remove Air Fry Basket from oven. Select DEHYDRATE, set temperature to 135°F, and set time to 8 hours.
2. Lightly spray the banana slices with lemon juice, spread in the Air Fry Basket in a single layer. Open door and install the basket in the top position level of the unit. Close door and begin cooking, flipping halfway through cooking.
3. When cooking is complete, carefully remove the banana chips from the oven. Enjoy!

Butternut Squash Fries

Serves 2

PREP TIME: 15 minutes
COOK TIME: 40 minutes

nonstick spray
2 pounds butternut squash, peeled and
cut into ½ inch strips
1 tsp. chili powder
½ tsp. ground cinnamon
¼ tsp. garlic salt

1. Remove Air Fry Basket from oven. Select AIR FRY, set temperature to 390°F, and set time to 20 minutes. Press the setting dial to begin preheating.
2. While unit is preheating, season butternut squash with all other ingredients in a medium bowl until well combined. Arrange half of the squash fries in the basket, making sure they are not crowding each other. Spray with nonstick spray.
3. When unit has preheated, open door, install the SearPlate in the bottom level of the unit and the basket in the top level of the unit. Close door to begin cooking, flipping halfway through cooking.
4. Repeat with the remaining fries.
5. When cooking is complete, carefully remove basket from the oven. Serve warm.

Bow Tie Pasta Chips

Serves 6

PREP TIME: 10 minutes
COOK TIME: 8 minutes

nonstick spray
2 cups white bow tie pasta
1 tbsp. nutritional yeast
1 tbsp. canola oil
1½ tsps. Italian seasoning blend
½ tsp. salt

1. Cook the pasta for ½ the time called for on the package. Toss the drained pasta with the canola oil, nutritional yeast, Italian seasoning, and salt.
2. Remove Air Fry Basket from oven. Select AIR FRY, set temperature to 390°F, and set time to 8 minutes. Press the setting dial to begin preheating.
3. While unit is preheating, arrange pasta in the basket, making sure they are not crowding each other. Spray with nonstick spray.
4. When unit has preheated, open door, install the SearPlate in the bottom level of the unit and the basket in the top level of the unit. Close door to begin cooking, shaking halfway through cooking.
5. When cooking is complete, carefully remove basket from the oven. Serve immediately.

Dried Mangoes

PREP TIME: 20 minutes
COOK TIME: 8 hours

spray bottle of lemon juice
2 large mangoes

1. Peel the mangoes; cut in 3/8-inch slices, then remove pit. Lightly spray with lemon juice.
2. Remove Air Fry Basket from oven. Select DEHYDRATE, set temperature to 135°F, and set time to 8 hours.
3. Place the mango slices in the Air Fry Basket in a single layer. Open door and install the basket in the top position level of the unit. Close door and begin cooking, flipping halfway through cooking.
4. When cooking is complete, carefully remove the mango from the oven. Enjoy!

Crispy Zucchini Fries

Serves 4

PREP TIME: 10 minutes
COOK TIME: 10 minutes

nonstick spray
1 pound zucchini, sliced into 2½-inch sticks
¾ cup panko breadcrumbs
Salt, to taste

1. Season the zucchini with salt and set aside for about 10 minutes.
2. Place breadcrumbs in a shallow dish and coat zucchini fries in it.
3. Remove Air Fry Basket from oven. Select AIR FRY, set temperature to 425°F, and set time to 10 minutes. Press the setting dial to begin preheating.
4. While unit is preheating, arrange the zucchini fries in the basket, making sure they are not crowding each other. Spray with nonstick spray.
5. When unit has preheated, open door, install the SearPlate in the bottom level of the unit and the basket in the top level of the unit. Close door to begin cooking, flipping halfway through cooking.
6. When cooking is complete, carefully remove basket from the oven. Serve warm.

Air Fried Zucchini Gratin

PREP TIME: 10 minutes COOK TIME: 15 minutes	nonstick spray 2 zucchinis, cut into 8 equal sized pieces 4 tbsps. Parmesan cheese, grated 2 tbsps. bread crumbs 1 tbsp. fresh parsley, chopped 1 tbsp. canola oil Salt and black pepper, to taste

1. Remove Air Fry Basket from oven. Select AIR FRY, set temperature to 390°F, and set time to 15 minutes. Press the setting dial to begin preheating.
2. While unit is preheating, arrange zucchini pieces in the basket with their skin side down, making sure they are not crowding each other. Top with the remaining ingredients and spray with nonstick spray.
3. When unit has preheated, open door, install the SearPlate in the bottom level of the unit and the basket in the top level of the unit. Close door to begin cooking, flipping halfway through cooking.
4. When cooking is complete, carefully remove basket from the oven. Serve warm.

Cheesy Jalapeño Poppers

PREP TIME: 5 minutes COOK TIME: 10 minutes	cooking spray 8 jalapeño peppers ¼ cup shredded Cheddar cheese ½ cup whipped cream cheese

1. Use a paring knife to carefully cut off the jalapeño tops, then scoop out the ribs and seeds. Set aside.
2. In a medium bowl, mix the cream cheese and Cheddar cheese. Place the mixture in a sealable plastic bag, and using a pair of scissors, cut off one corner from the bag. Gently squeeze the cream cheese mixture into each pepper until almost full. Spray with cooking spray.
3. Remove SearPlate from oven. Select BROIL, set temperature to LO, and set time to 10 minutes.
4. Place the poppers in the SearPlate. Open door and install the SearPlate in the bottom level of the unit. Close door and begin cooking, until the cheese is melted.
5. When cooking is complete, carefully remove SearPlate from the oven. Let the poppers cool for 5 to 10 minutes before serving.

Crunchy Spicy Chickpeas

PREP TIME: 5 minutes
COOK TIME: 20 minutes

225 g large okras
15 g coconut, grated freshly
30 g chickpea flour
¼ of onion, chopped
1 tsp. garam masala powder
½ tsp. red chilli powder

½ tsp. ground turmeric
½ tsp. ground cumin
Salt, to taste

1. Remove Air Fry Basket from oven Select AIR FRY, set temperature to 390°F, and set time to 10 minutes. Press the setting dial to begin preheating.
2. While unit is preheating, mix together all the ingredients in a medium bowl and toss to coat well.
3. Arrange half of the chickpeas in the basket, making sure they are not crowding each other. Spray with nonstick spray.
4. When unit has preheated, open door, install the SearPlate in the bottom level of the unit and the basket in the top level of the unit. Close door to begin cooking, flipping halfway through cooking.
5. Repeat with the remaining chickpeas.
6. When cooking is complete, carefully remove basket from the oven. Serve immediately.

Nutty Cauliflower Poppers

PREP TIME: 10 minutes
COOK TIME: 14 minutes

¼ cup golden raisins
1 cup boiling water
¼ cup toasted pine nuts
1 head of cauliflower, cut into small florets
½ cup canola oil, divided
1 tbsp. curry powder
¼ tsp. salt

1. Put the raisins in boiling water in a bowl and set aside.
2. Drizzle 1 tsp. canola oil on the pine nuts in another bowl.
3. Mix together cauliflower, salt, curry powder and remaining canola oil.
4. Install SearPlate in the bottom level of the unit, then close the door. Select AIR ROAST, set temperature to 390°F, and set time to 14 minutes. Press the setting dial to begin preheating.
5. When unit has preheated, open door and use oven mitts to remove SearPlate and place it on top of oven. Transfer cauliflower to the SearPlate.
6. Reinstall the SearPlate in the bottom level of the unit. Close door to begin cooking.
7. After 12 minutes, open door and add the pine nuts onto the SearPlate. Close door to finish cooking.
8. When cooking is complete, carefully remove SearPlate from oven with oven mitts. Transfer the cauliflower and pine nuts to a serving bowl, stir well. Drain and top with raisins. Serve warm.

CHAPTER 10

DESSERT

Walnut Brownies

PREP TIME: 10 minutes
COOK TIME: 22 minutes

½ cup chocolate, chopped roughly
⅓ cup butter
¼ cup walnuts, chopped
1 large egg, beaten
5 tbsps. sugar

5 tbsps. self-rising flour
1 tsp. vanilla extract
Pinch of salt

1. Line a baking pan with greased parchment paper.
2. Microwave chocolate and butter on high for 2 minutes.
3. Mix the sugar, egg, vanilla extract, salt and chocolate mixture in a small bowl until well combined.
4. Stir in the flour mixture gently and fold in the walnuts.
5. Pour the mixture into the baking pan and smooth the top surface of mixture with the back of spatula.
6. Install rack in bottom position, then close door. Select BAKE, set temperature to 355°F, and set time to 20 minutes. Press the setting dial to begin preheating.
7. When unit has preheated, open door and place the baking pan onto the center of the rack. Close door to begin cooking.
8. After 20 minutes, check brownies for doneness by sticking a toothpick in the center of the brownies. If it comes out clean, remove from oven.
9. When cooking is complete, carefully remove pan from the oven. Cut into 8 equal sized squares to serve.

Chocolate Molten Cake

PREP TIME: 5 minutes
COOK TIME: 10 minutes

2 eggs
3.5 ounces (99 g) butter, melted
3.5 ounces (99 g) chocolate, melted
3½ tbsps. sugar
1½ tbsps. flour

1. Grease four ramekins with a little butter.
2. Mix the eggs, butter and sugar rigorously, then stir in the melted chocolate.
3. Slowly fold in the flour. Spoon an equal amount of the mixture into each ramekin.
4. Install rack in bottom position, then close door. Select BAKE, set temperature to 375°F, and set time to 10 minutes. Press the setting dial to begin preheating.
5. When unit has preheated, open door and place ramekins onto the center of the rack. Close door to begin cooking.
6. After 10 minutes, check the cakes for doneness by sticking a toothpick in the center of the cakes. If it comes out clean, remove from oven.
7. When cooking is complete, carefully remove from the oven. Put the ramekins upside-down on plates and let the cakes fall out. Serve hot.

Stuffed Apples

PREP TIME: 10 minutes
COOK TIME: 13 minutes

4 small firm apples, cored
½ cup whipped cream
½ cup blanched almonds
½ cup golden raisins
4 tbsps. sugar, divided
½ tsp. vanilla extract

1. Grease a baking dish lightly.
2. Put raisins, almond and half of sugar in a food processor and pulse until chopped.
3. Stuff each apple with the raisin mixture and arrange the apples in the prepared baking dish.
4. Install rack in bottom position, then close door. Select BAKE, set temperature to 355°F, and set time to 10 minutes. Press the setting dial to begin preheating.
5. When unit has preheated, open door and place baking dish onto the center of the rack. Close door to begin cooking.
6. When cooking is complete, carefully remove dish from the oven.
7. Add the cream, remaining sugar and vanilla extract on medium heat in a pan and cook for about 3 minutes, continuously stirring.
8. Turn off the heat and serve apple with vanilla sauce.

Red Velvet Cupcakes

PREP TIME: 15 minutes
COOK TIME: 12 minutes

For the Cupcakes:
3 eggs
2 cups refined flour
¾ cup icing sugar
¾ cup peanut butter
2 tsps. beet powder
1 tsp. cocoa powder

For the Frosting:
1 cup cream cheese
1 cup butter
¾ cup icing sugar
¼ cup strawberry sauce
1 tsp. vanilla essence

1. Mix all the cupcakes ingredients in a large bowl until well combined.
2. Transfer the mixture into silicon cups and place in a baking pan.
3. Install rack in bottom position, then close door. Select BAKE, set temperature to 340°F, and set time to 12 minutes. Press the setting dial to begin preheating.
4. When unit has preheated, open door and place pan onto the center of the rack. Close door to begin cooking.
5. After 12 minutes, check cupcakes for doneness by sticking a toothpick in the center of the cupcakes. If it comes out clean, remove from oven.
6. When cooking is complete, carefully remove pan from the oven.
7. Mix all the frosting ingredients in a large bowl until well combined. Top each cupcake evenly with frosting and serve.

Chocolate Croissants

PREP TIME: 5 minutes
COOK TIME: 16 minutes

cooking spray
1 sheet frozen puff pastry, thawed
1 large egg, beaten
⅓ cup chocolate-hazelnut spread

1. Install SearPlate in the bottom level of the unit, then close the door. Select RAPID BAKE, set temperature to 375°F, and set the time to 8 minutes.
2. On a lightly floured surface, roll puff pastry into a 14-inch square. Cut pastry into quarters to form 4 squares. Cut each square diagonally to form 8 triangles.
3. Spread 2 tsps. chocolate-hazelnut spread on each triangle; from wider end, roll up pastry. Brush egg on top of each roll. Spray with cooking spray.
4. When unit has preheated, open the door, carefully remove the SearPlate with oven mitts, and place on top of the oven. Carefully place half of rolls on the SearPlate. Reinstall the SearPlate in the bottom level of the unit and close the door to begin cooking, until pastry is golden brown.
5. Repeat with the remaining rolls.
6. When cooking is complete, remove SearPlate and let ool on a wire rack. Serve warm.

Sweet Potato Pie

PREP TIME: 5 minutes
COOK TIME: 1 hour

1 (9-inch) prepared frozen pie dough, thawed
6-ounce sweet potato
2 large eggs
¼ cup heavy cream
1 tbsp. butter, melted
1 tsp. canola oil

2 tbsps. maple syrup
1 tbsp. light brown sugar
¾ tsp. vanilla extract
½ tsp. ground cinnamon
⅛ tsp. ground nutmeg
Salt, to taste

1. Install SearPlate in the bottom level of the unit, then close the door. Select AIR ROAST, set temperature to 400°F, and set time to 30 minutes. Press the setting dial to begin preheating.
2. When unit has preheated, open door and use oven mitts to remove SearPlate and place it on top of oven. Rub the sweet potato with oil and transfer to the SearPlate.
3. Reinstall the SearPlate in the bottom level of the unit. Close door to begin cooking.
4. When cooking is complete, carefully remove SearPlate from oven with oven mitts.
5. Let the sweet potato cool and mash it completely.
6. Add rest of the ingredients and mix until well combined.
7. Add the filling to the center of the dough, leaving a 2-inch rim around the perimeter free of filling. Fold the edges of the dough up and over the filling 6 times, leaving the center open.
8. Install SearPlate in the bottom level of the unit, then close the door. Select RAPID BAKE, set temperature to 400°F, and set the time to 30 minutes.
9. When unit has preheated, open the door, carefully remove the SearPlate with oven mitts, and place on top of the oven. Carefully place dough on the SearPlate. Reinstall the SearPlate in the bottom level of the unit and close the door to begin cooking.
10. When cooking is complete, remove SearPlate from the oven. Serve warm.

Rich Chocolate Cookie

PREP TIME: 10 minutes
COOK TIME: 9 minutes

Nonstick baking spray with flour
3 tbsps. softened butter
1/3 cup plus 1 tbsp. brown sugar
1/2 cup flour
1 egg yolk
3/4 cup chocolate chips
2 tbsps. ground white chocolate

1/4 tsp. baking soda
1/2 tsp. vanilla

1. In a medium bowl, beat the butter and brown sugar together until fluffy. Stir in the egg yolk.
2. Add the flour, white chocolate, baking soda and vanilla, and combine well. Stir in the chocolate chips.
3. Line a baking pan with parchment paper. Spray the parchment paper with nonstick baking spray with flour.
4. Spread the batter into the prepared pan, leaving a 1/2-inch border on all sides.
5. Install rack in bottom position, then close door. Select BAKE, set temperature to 350°F, and set time to 9 minutes. Press the setting dial to begin preheating.
6. When unit has preheated, open door and place pan onto the center of the rack. Close door to begin cooking, until the cookie is light brown and just barely set.
7. When cooking is complete, carefully remove pan from the oven. Let cool for 10 minutes. Remove the cookie from the pan, remove the parchment paper, and let cool on a wire rack. Serve immediately.

Shortbread Fingers

Serves 10

PREP TIME: 10 minutes
COOK TIME: 12 minutes

nonstick spray
1 2/3 cups plain flour
1/3 cup caster sugar
3/4 cup butter

1. Line a baking pan with parchment paper. Spray the parchment paper with nonstick spray.
2. Mix sugar, flour and butter in a bowl to form a dough.
3. Cut the dough into 10 equal sized fingers and prick the fingers lightly with a fork.
4. Transfer the fingers to the lined baking pan.
5. Install rack in bottom position, then close door. Select BAKE, set temperature to 355°F, and set time to 12 minutes. Press the setting dial to begin preheating.
6. When unit has preheated, open door and place pan onto the center of the rack. Close door to begin cooking.
7. When cooking is complete, carefully remove pan from the oven. Serve warm.

Spice Cookies

PREP TIME: 15 minutes
COOK TIME: 12 minutes

nonstick spray
4 tbsps. (½ stick) unsalted butter, at room temperature
2 tbsps. agave nectar
1 large egg
2½ cups almond flour
½ cup sugar
2 tbsps. water
2 tsps. ground ginger

1 tsp. baking soda
1 tsp. ground cinnamon
½ tsp. freshly grated nutmeg
¼ tsp. kosher salt

1. Line a baking pan with parchment paper. Spray the parchment paper with nonstick spray.
2. In a large bowl, beat together the butter, agave, egg, and water with a hand mixer on medium speed until fluffy.
3. Add the almond flour, sugar, ginger, cinnamon, nutmeg, baking soda, and salt. Beat on low speed until well combined.
4. Roll the dough into 2-tbsp. balls and arrange them on the baking pan.
5. Install rack in bottom position, then close door. Select BAKE, set temperature to 325°F, and set time to 12 minutes. Press the setting dial to begin preheating.
6. When unit has preheated, open door and place pan onto the center of the rack. Close door to begin cooking, until the tops of cookies are lightly browned.
7. When cooking is complete, carefully remove pan from the oven. Transfer the cookies to a wire rack and let cool completely. Serve immediately

Pineapple and Chocolate Cake

PREP TIME: 10 minutes
COOK TIME: 35 minutes

2 cups flour
1 large egg
½ pound (227 g) pineapple, chopped
½ cup pineapple juice
4 ounces (113 g) butter, melted
1 ounce (28 g) dark chocolate, grated
¼ cup sugar
2 tbsps. skimmed milk

1. Grease a cake tin with a little butter.
2. In a medium bowl, combine the butter and flour to create a crumbly consistency.
3. Add the sugar, chopped pineapple, juice and grated dark chocolate and mix well.
4. In a separate bowl, pour in the egg and milk. Add this mixture to the flour mixture and stir well until a soft dough forms.
5. Install rack in bottom position, then close door. Select BAKE, set temperature to 370°F, and set time to 35 minutes. Press the setting dial to begin preheating.
6. When unit has preheated, open door and place the cake tin onto the center of the rack. Close door to begin cooking.
7. After 35 minutes, check cake for doneness by sticking a toothpick in the center of the cake. If it comes out clean, remove from oven.
8. When cooking is complete, carefully remove the tin from the oven. Serve immediately.

APPENDIX 1:
Basic Kitchen Conversions & Equivalents

DRY MEASUREMENTS CONVERSION CHART

3 teaspoons = 1 tablespoon = 1/16 cup

6 teaspoons = 2 tablespoons = 1/8 cup

12 teaspoons = 4 tablespoons = ¼ cup

24 teaspoons = 8 tablespoons = ½ cup

36 teaspoons = 12 tablespoons = ¾ cup

48 teaspoons = 16 tablespoons = 1 cup

METRIC TO US COOKING CONVERSIONS

OVEN TEMPERATURES

120 ºC = 250 ºF

160 ºC = 320 ºF

180 ºC = 350 ºF

205 ºC = 400 ºF

220 ºC = 425 ºF

LIQUID MEASUREMENTS CONVERSION CHART

8 fluid ounces = 1 cup = ½ pint = ¼ quart

16 fluid ounces = 2 cups = 1 pint = ½ quart

32 fluid ounces = 4 cups = 2 pints = 1 quart = ¼ gallon

128 fluid ounces = 16 cups = 8 pints = 4 quarts = 1 gallon

BAKING IN GRAMS

1 cup flour = 140 grams

1 cup sugar = 150 grams

1 cup powdered sugar = 160 grams

1 cup heavy cream = 235 grams

VOLUME

1 milliliter = 1/5 tsp

5 ml = 1 tsp

15 ml = 1 tbsp

240 ml = 1 cup or 8 fluid ounces

1 liter = 34 fluid ounces

WEIGHT

1 gram = .035 ounces

100 grams = 3.5 ounces

500 grams = 1.1 pounds

1 kilogram = 35 ounces

US TO METRIC COOKING CONVERSIONS

1/5 tsp = 1 ml

1 tsp = 5 ml

1 tbsp = 15 ml

1 fluid ounces = 30 ml

1 cup = 237 ml

1 pint (2 cups) = 473 ml

1 quart (4 cups) = .95 liter

1 gallon (16 cups) = 3.8 liters

1 oz = 28 grams

1 pound = 454 grams

BUTTER

1 cup butter = 2 sticks = 8 ounces = 230 grams = 16 tablespoons

WHAT DOES 1 CUP EQUAL

1 cup = 8 fluid ounces

1 cup = 16 tablespoons

1 cup = 48 teaspoons

1 cup = ½ pint

1 cup = ¼ quart

1 cup = 1/16 gallon

1 cup = 240 ml

BAKING PAN CONVERSIONS

9-inch round cake pan = 12 cups

10-inch tube pan =16 cups

10-inch bundt pan = 12 cups

9-inch springform pan = 10 cups

9 x 5 inch loaf pan = 8 cups

9-inch square pan = 8 cups

BAKING PAN CONVERSIONS

1 cup all-purpose flour = 4.5 oz

1 cup rolled oats = 3 oz

1 large egg = 1.7 oz

1 cup butter = 8 oz

1 cup milk = 8 oz

1 cup heavy cream = 8.4 oz

1 cup granulated sugar = 7.1 oz

1 cup packed brown sugar = 7.75 oz

1 cup vegetable oil = 7.7 oz

1 cup unsifted powdered sugar = 4.4 oz

APPENDIX 2:
NINJA FOODI DUAL HEAT AIR FRYER OVEN TIMETABLE

RAPID BAKE CHART

INGREDIENT	AMOUNT	PREPARATION	TEMP	TIME
Premade cinnamon rolls (refrigerated)	1 tube (8 rolls)	Follow directions on package	Recommended Temp on package	10-13 mins
Store-bought chocolate chip cookie dough	1 package (12 cookies)	Follow directions on package	Recommended Temp on package	6-8 mins
Store-bought sugar cookie dough	1 package (12 cookies)	Follow directions on package	Recommended Temp on package	7-9 mins
Store-bought biscuits (refrigerated)	1 tube (8 biscuits)	Follow directions on package	Recommended Temp on package	9-11 mins
Boxed coffee cake mix	1 box	Follow directions on package	Recommended Temp on package	20-22 mins
Crescent rolls (refrigerated)	1 tube (8 rolls)	Follow directions on package	Recommended Temp on package	6-9 mins
9-inch apple pie (frozen)	1 pie	N/A	Reduce recommended Temp on package by 25°F	28-32 mins
Boxed cornbread mix	1 box	Follow directions on package	Reduce recommended Temp on package by 25°F	15-20 mins
Boxed brownie mix	1 box	Follow directions on package	Reduce recommended Temp on package by 25°F	20-25 mins
Boxed banana bread mix	1 box	Follow directions on package	Reduce recommended Temp on package by 25°F	40-45 mins
Individual frozen pot pie	1 pie	N/A	Reduce recommended Temp on package by 25°F	15-25 mins
Family-sized frozen pot pie	1 pie	N/A	Reduce recommended Temp on package by 25°F	30-40 mins
Dinner rolls (frozen)	8 rolls	N/A	Recommended Temp on package	5-8 mins
Puff pastry shells (frozen)	6 shells	N/A	Recommended Temp on package	8-12 mins
Turnovers (frozen)	4 turnovers	N/A	Recommended Temp on package	10-14 mins
Sandwich pockets (frozen)	2 pockets	N/A	Recommended Temp on package	18-20 mins

AIR FRY COOKING CHART

INGREDIENT	AMOUNT	PREPARATION	TEMP	TIME
FROZEN FOOD				
Chicken nuggets	2 boxes (24 oz)	None	400°F	26-30 mins
Chicken thighs	8 thighs (8-10 oz each)	None	390°F	26-30 mins
Chicken wings	2 lbs	None	400°F	24-28 mins
Egg Rolls	Up to 2 lbs	None	360°F	18-20 mins
Fish fillets	1 package (10 fillets)	None	400°F	16-18 mins
Fish sticks	1 box (16 oz)	None	400°F	14-16 mins
French fries	16 oz	None	390°F	22-24 mins
Mozzarella sticks	Up to 2 lbs	None	375°F	10-15 mins
Pizza Rolls	Up to 2 lbs	None	375°F	10-13 mins
Popcorn shrimp	Up to 2 lbs	None	390°F	10-11 mins
Pot stickers	3 bag (30 count)	None	390°F	14-18 mins
Tater tots	2 lbs	None	360°F	20-25 mins
MEAT, POULTRY, FISH				
Bacon	½ package (8 oz)	None	390°F	7-10 mins
Burgers	5 ¼-lb patties, 80% lean	1 inch thick	375°F	10-12 mins
Chicken drumsticks	6 drumsticks	Pat dry	400°F	22-35 mins
Chicken thighs, bone in, skin on	5 thighs (4-6 oz each)	Pat dry	390°F	22-28 mins
Chicken wings	2 lbs	Pat dry	400°F	28-30 mins
Crab cakes	8 cakes (6-8 oz each)	None	400°F	12-17 mins
Salmon fillets	6-8 fillets (6-8 oz each)	None	400°F	15-20 mins
Sausages	10 sausages (3 oz each)	None	390°F	15-20 mins
Shrimp, peeled	2 lbs	Pat dry	390°F	7-10 mins
VEGETABLES				
Asparagus	Up to 2 lbs	Trim stems	400°F	8-10 mins
Beets	1.5 lbs	Peel, cut in ½-inch cubes	390°F	28-30 mins
Bell peppers (for roasting)	4 peppers	Cut in quarters, remove seeds	425°F	15-20 mins
Broccoli	Up to 2 lbs	Cut in 1-2-inch florets	375°F	15-17 mins
Carrots	1 lb	Peel, cut in ¼-inch rounds	425°F	15-20 mins
Cauliflower	Up to 2 lbs	Cut in 1-2-inch florets	390°F	15-18 mins
Corn on the cob	7 ears	Whole ears, remove husks	400°F	14-17 mins
Green beans	Up to 2 lbs	Stems trimmed	425°F	10-12 mins
Kale (for chips)	4 oz	Tear into pieces, remove stem	325°F	8-10 mins
Mushrooms	16 oz	Rinse, slice thinly	390°F	20-25 mins
Potato Wedges	Up to 2 lbs	Cut in 1-inch wedges	390°F	28-31 mins
Potatoes, russet	1 lb	Hand-cut fries, soak 20 mins in cold water, then pat dry	410°F	25-30 mins
Potatoes, sweet	1 lb	Hand-cut fries, soak 30 mins in cold water, then pat dry	400°F	25-28 mins
Yellow Squash	2 lbs	Cut in ¼ lengthwise then in 1-inch pieces	400°F	12-15 mins
Zucchini	2 lbs	Cut in ¼ lengthwise then in 1-inch pieces	400°F	12-15 mins

GRIDDLE CHART

INGREDIENT	AMOUNT	PREPARATION	TEMP	TIME
Griddled cheese sandwich	1 sandwich	As desired	375°F	5-7 mins
Pancakes	4 pancakes (4 inches wide)	As desired	375°F	4-6 mins
French toast	4 slices	As desired	375°F	5-7 mins
Over-easy eggs	6 eggs	As desired	375°F	2-6 mins
Quesadillas	1 quesadilla	As desired	375°F	5-7 mins
Pre-cut fajita vegetables	12 ounces	Pre-cut, thin strips	375°F	10-15 mins
Crab cakes (refrigerated)	4 cakes (10 oz total)	N/A	425°F	8-10 mins
Crab cakes (frozen)	2 cakes (6 oz total)	N/A	425°F	15-18 mins
Hash browns (frozen)	About 4 cups	N/A	425°F	10-15 mins
Pot stickers (frozen)	1 bag (5 oz)	Place flat on tray with ½ cup water	425°F	8-12 mins
Hot dogs	8 hot dogs	N/A	425°F	5-8 mins

DEHYDRATE CHART

INGREDIENTS	PREPARATION	TEMP	TIME
FRUITS & VEGETABLES			
Apples	Cut in ⅛-inch slices, remove core, rinse in lemon water, pat dry	135°F	7-8 hrs
Asparagus	Cut in 1-inch pieces, blanch	135°F	6-8 hrs
Bananas	Peel, cut in ⅜-inch slices	135°F	8-10 hrs
Beets	Peel, cut in ⅛-inch slices	135°F	7-8 hrs
Eggplant	Peel, cut in ¼-inch slices, blanch	135°F	6-8 hrs
Fresh herbs	Rinse, pat dry, remove stems	135°F	4-6 hrs
Ginger root	Cut in ⅜-inch slices	135°F	6 hrs
Mangoes	Peel, cut in ⅜-inch slices, remove pit	135°F	6-8 hrs
Mushrooms	Cleaned with soft brush (do not wash)	135°F	6-8 hrs
Pineapple	Peel, cut in ⅜-½-inch slices, remove core	135°F	6-8 hrs
Strawberries	Cut in half or in ½-inch slices	135°F	6-8 hrs
Tomatoes	Cut in ⅜-inch slices or grate; steam if planning to rehydrate	135°F	6-8 hrs
MEAT, POULTRY, FISH			
Beef jerky	Cut in ¼-inch slices, remove all fat, marinate 8-24 hrs	150°F	5-7 hrs
Chicken jerky	Cut in ¼-inch slices, marinate overnight	150°F	5-7 hrs
Salmon jerky	Cut in ¼-inch slices, marinate overnight	150°F	5-7 hrs
Turkey jerky	Cut in ¼-inch slices, marinate overnight	150°F	5-8 hrs

APPENDIX 3: Recipes Index

Made in the USA
Las Vegas, NV
31 October 2023

80032373R00044